66

"SIGNS"
OF AN IMMINENT MASS DEPARTURE

BY
H. D. WILLIAMS, M.D., PH.D.

> **Disclaimer**
>
> The author of this work has quoted the writers of many articles and books. This does not mean that the author endorses or recommends the works of others. If the author quotes someone, it does not mean that he agrees with all of the author's tenets, statements, concepts, or words, whether in the work quoted or any other work of the author. There has been no attempt to alter the meaning of the quotes; and therefore, some of the quotes are long in order to give the entire sense of the passage.

Copyright © 2019 by H. D. Williams
All Rights Reserved
Printed in the United States of America

Library of Congress Control Number:

REL015000: Religion: Christianity – History General.

ISBN 978-1-7321746-7-2

All Scripture quotes are from the King James Bible except those verses compared and then the source is identified.

No part of this work may be reproduced without the expressed consent of the publisher, except for brief quotes, whether by electronic, photocopying, recording, or information storage and retrieval systems.

Address All Inquiries To:
THE OLD PATHS PUBLICATIONS, Inc.
142 Gold Flume Way
Cleveland, Georgia, U.S.A. 30528

Web: www.theoldpathspublications.com
E-mail: TOP@theoldpathspublications.com

**The cover depicts a "blood moon" that often occurs on special Jewish days.
[Joel 2:31, Acts 2:20, Rev. 6:12]**

DEDICATION

This book is dedicated to those who are "looking for the blessed hope and glorious appearing of the Great God and our Saviour" and who shall receive the "crown of rejoicing."

> **Tit 2:13** *Looking for that blessed hope, and the glorious appearing of the great God and our Saviour Jesus Christ;*

> **1Th 2:19** *For what is our hope, or joy, or crown of rejoicing? Are not even ye in the presence of our Lord Jesus Christ at his coming?*

66 SIGNS OF AN IMMINENT MASS DEPARTURE

PREFACE

What is the state of Christendom today? Several Bible passages come to mind. The first one is Paul urging his young preacher friend Timothy –

> *"I charge thee therefore before God, and the Lord Jesus Christ, who shall judge the quick and the dead at his appearing and his kingdom; 2 Preach the word; be instant in season, out of season; reprove, rebuke, exhort with all longsuffering and doctrine. 3 For the time will come when they will not endure sound doctrine; but after their own lusts shall they heap to themselves teachers, having itching ears; 4 And they shall turn away their ears from the truth, and shall be turned unto fables."*
> *(2 Timothy 4:1-4).*

I believe we are living in that day of doctrinal compromise. People want sermons that are non-judgmental and non-directive. They want "feel good" sermons. They want "cotton candy" sermons that are sweet but have no substance. This kind of preaching makes the hearers ripe for the deception of the evil one!

The next passage that comes to mind is 2 Peter 3:3-4 –

> *"Knowing this first, that there shall come in the last days scoffers, walking after their own lusts, 4 And saying, Where is the promise of his coming? for since the fathers fell asleep, all things continue as they were from the beginning of the creation."*

66 SIGNS OF AN IMMINENT MASS DEPARTURE

Too many professing Christians are so busy doing their own thing that they give little or no thought to the end time events that are falling into place right before their eyes! Others scoff at the truth that the next event on God's Prophetic Calendar is the RAPTURE! In short too many Christians are spiritually ASLEEP.

Dr. H.D. Williams is sounding the WAKE-UP CALL!

> *"Knowing the time, that now it is high time to awake out of sleep: for now is our salvation nearer than when we believed."*

In this book, **66 "Signs" Of An Imminent Departure From Earth,** Brother Williams reveals 66 evidences that Jesus is coming back soon to receive His own! ARE YOU READY?

The greatest thing about this book is that each point in this book is framed in a concise manner, clearly demonstrating that Jesus IS Coming soon! It is not meant to be an academic work but to motivate Christians to get busy for the Lord for "the night is far spent."

66 "Signs" Of An Imminent Mass Departure will open your eyes to the lateness of the hour. It is worthy of your time and attention and definitely a book to share with your friends and family.

Until The Shout,
Dr. David L Brown
Pastor, First Baptist Church, Oak Creek, Wisconsin)
President – King James Bible Research Council
Author of "The Indestructible Book"
Curator of the "Biblical Heritage Archive Museum"

66 SIGNS OF AN IMMINENT MASS DEPARTURE

TABLE OF CONTENTS

DEDICATION 3
PREFACE 4
TABLE OF CONTENTS 6
INTRODUCTION 10
SIGN #1 24
    ARTIFICIALLY INTELLIGENT (AI) ROBOTS 24
SIGN #2 26
    TECHNOLOGY ALLOWING THE MARK OF THE BEAST 26
SIGN #3 28
    GLOBAL TECHNOLOGY AND THE SPREAD OF THE GOSPEL . 28
SIGN #4 29
    GLOBAL COMMUNICATIONS 29
SIGN #5 30
    GLOBAL CALLS FOR PEACE 30
SIGN #6 31
    GLOBAL TRAVEL 31
SIGN #7 32
    GLOBAL PERSECUTIONS OF BELIEVERS 32
SIGN #8 33
    GLOBAL EXPLOSION IN KNOWLEDGE 33
SIGN #9 34
    GLOBAL EXPLOSION IN SELFITIS 34
SIGN #10 35
    GLOBAL EXPLOSION IN IMMORALITY 35
SIGN #11 36
    GLOBAL EXPLOSION IN PORNOGRAPHY 36
SIGN #12 37
    GLOBAL EMERGING CHURCH 37
SIGN #13 38
    GLOBAL ABANDONMENT OF THE BIBLE 38
SIGN #14 39
    GLOBAL REWRITING OF THE BIBLE 39
SIGN #15 40
    THE GLOBAL OR ONE WORLD BIBLE 40
SIGN #16 41
    GLOBAL APOSTASY 41
SIGN #17 42
    THE GLOBAL LEADER (Antichrist) 42
SIGN #18 43
    GLOBAL PESTILENCES 43

66 SIGNS OF AN IMMINENT MASS DEPARTURE

SIGN #19 44
   THE GLOBAL GOVERNMENT 44
SIGN #20 45
   THE GLOBAL REGATHERING OF ISRAEL 45
SIGN #21 46
   THE GLOBALLY OCCURRING EARTHQUAKES 46
SIGN #22 47
   THE GLOBAL LAWLESSNESS 47
SIGN #23 49
   GLOBALLY DROUGHTS & FAMINE INCREASING 49
SIGN #24 50
   GLOBAL FALSE PROPHET(S) 50
SIGN #25 51
   GLOBAL NUCLEAR DISASTER 51
SIGN #26 53
   GLOBALLY LOVE WAXING COLD 53
SIGN #27 54
   GLOBAL DECLINE OF THE WEST 54
SIGN #28 55
   GLOBAL UNUSUAL WEATHER 55
SIGN #29 56
   GLOBAL SPIRITUAL BLINDNESS 56
SIGN #30 57
   BLINDNESS OF ISRAEL 57
SIGN #31 58
   ISRAEL DECLARED A NATION 58
SIGN #32 59
   ISRAEL SUPERNATURALLY PROTECTED 59
SIGN #33 60
   ISRAEL AND ANTISEMITISM 60
SIGN #34 61
   ISRAEL'S CAPITOL IS AGAIN JERUSALEM 61
SIGN #35 63
   ISRAEL'S 3rd TEMPLE 63
SIGN #36 65
   IMPLEMENTS HAVE BEEN MADE FOR THE 3rd TEMPLE 65
SIGN #37 75
   ISRAEL'S DEDICATION OF THE ALTAR FOR THE 3rd TEMPLE 75
SIGN #38 77
   THE EASTERN GATE IS SHUT UNTIL… 77
SIGN #39 78
   OFFERINGS BEGINNING FOR THE 3rd TEMPLE 78

66 SIGNS OF AN IMMINENT MASS DEPARTURE

SIGN #40 79
   ISRAEL IS BOOMING, BLOOMING, & PROSPERING............ 79
SIGN #41 81
   THE SANHEDRIN HAS BEEN REFORMED........................ 81
SIGN #42 82
   THE FAULT LINE IN THE MOUNT OF OLIVES 82
SIGN #43 83
   THE DEAD SEA IS CHANGING 83
SIGN #44 84
   THE FALSE REPLACEMENT THEOLOGY 84
SIGN #45 85
   RAMPANT SEXUAL IMMORALITY 85
SIGN #46 86
   MARRIAGE WOULD BE DISDAINED 86
SIGN #47 87
   NATIONS PLANNING TO ATTACK ISRAEL 87
SIGN #48 88
   RUSSIA'S INVOLVEMENT IN THE MIDDLE EAST 88
SIGN #49 90
   DAMASCUS WILL BE DESTROYED................................... 90
SIGN #50 91
   GOD'S PROTECTION OF ISRAEL 91
SIGN #51 92
   THE RISE OF ASIA (CHINA).. 92
SIGN #52 93
   SORROWS 93
SIGN #53 94
   POPULATION EXPLOSION 94
SIGN #54 95
   IRAN (PERSIA) 95
SIGN #55 97
   TURKEY (GOMER)... 97
SIGN #56 98
   LITERAL FULFILLMENT OF PROPHECIES 98
SIGN #57 99
   SIGNS IN THE HEAVENS 99
SIGN #58 100
   SCOFFERS MOCKING THE 2ND COMING........................ 100
SIGN #59 101
   EXPLOSION IN WITCHCRAFT... 101
SIGN #60 102
   REVIVAL OF THE HEBREW LANGUAGE 102

66 SIGNS OF AN IMMINENT MASS DEPARTURE

SIGN #61 103
    CALLING EVIL GOOD AND GOOD EVIL 103
SIGN #62 104
    DRUGS 104
SIGN #63 106
    GLOBAL BLASPHEMERS 106
SIGN #64 108
    DEMONIC EXPLOSION 108
SIGN #65 109
    LGBTQ AGENDA 109
SIGN #66 110
    WARS AND RUMOURS OF WARS 110
ABOUT THE AUTHOR 111

66 SIGNS OF AN IMMINENT MASS DEPARTURE

INTRODUCTION

As I sat down to write this "Introduction" for "Signs," I quickly checked the news and was amazed at some of the headlines:

1. **"Alabama Police Department Blames Satan for Spike in Homicides."** The article detailed a spike in homicides by "young people" who had turned away from God and "embraced Satan."
[https://www.al.com/news/2018/12/alabama-police-department-blames-satan-for-spike-in-homicides.html, accessed 12/2018]

2. **"Putin Issues Ominous Warning on Rising Nuclear War Threat."** The article said that while speaking at his annual news conference, Putin warned that, "it could lead to the destruction of civilization as a whole and maybe even our planet."
[https://apnews.com/deaa45c70d3c4da98410d5a3ec30951, accessed 12/2018]

3. **"John of Prison? Police Charge Brazilian Spiritual Healer…"** This article highlights the sexual immorality "charges against a popular Brazilian spiritual healer [called John of God] accused by hundreds of sex crimes."
[https://www.apnews.com/61f2e2fa376e4898aad1a4a3ac2ec308, accessed 12/2018]

4. **"Walgreens Employee Fatally Shoots Man After Photos Dispute."** The incident and tragedy occurred over a few "photos."
[http://www.fox5ny.com/news/walgreens-photo-dispute-shooting-ok, accessed 12/2018]

66 SIGNS OF AN IMMINENT MASS DEPARTURE

5. **"Ring of Fire Volcanoes Erupting is Biblical Sign of END OF DAYS, Claims Rabbi."** The article continued, "Rabbis have suggested the apparent increase in activity this year could show the world is heading for the end of days as laid out the Hebrew Bible…Rabbi Yosef Berger said, "This is a global phenomenon, clear for everyone to see, but the important message is for each individual to understand what is happening as part of the Messiah… Judaism's end of days heralds the coming of the Jewish Messiah. He will rule during the Messianic Age which will see the end of the world as we know it – ushering in the kingdom of God." Rabbi Nir Ben Artzi claimed he believes the Messiah is waiting to reveal himself – and linked his arrival to the volcanic eruptions. It was claimed earlier this year the Jewish Messiah had been born and the world was on the cusp of "redemption."
   [https://www.dailystar.co.uk/news/weird-news/749234/ring-of-fire-volcano-bible-prophecy-end-of-the-world-rabbi-prediction-hebrew, accessed 12/2018]

6. **"Boise Priest Who Lived in 'World of Satanism and Pornography' Sentenced to 25 Years in Prison."** The account said, "Faucher, 73, was accused of amassing thousands of child porn images and videos on his home computer — and pleaded guilty in September to sharing some of those images online. He apologized in the courtroom ahead of his sentencing at the Ada

County Courthouse in Boise on Thursday." [https://www.idahostatesman.com/news/local/crime/article223358745.html, accessed 12/2018]

7. **"Witchcraft Moves to the Mainstream in America as Christianity Declines - and has Trump in its Sights"** This article states, "Witchcraft is thriving in the US, with an estimated 1.5 million Americans now identifying as witches - more than the total number of Presbyterians. As Christianity declines across the country, paganism has swung to the mainstream, with witchcraft paraphernalia for sale on every high street and practises normalised across popular culture. In the past two years, it has also become darkly politicised."
[https://sg.news.yahoo.com/witchcraft-moves-mainstream-america-christianity-130445984.html, accessed 12/2018]

There were many more headlines on this ONE day and other recent days, which reveal that the 66 signs reported in this book gained from Bible texts and highlighted by current news articles are accurate. For many, the whole world seems "upside-down" and chaos seems to be spreading across our globe. Rioting, looting, burning and rock-throwing are now the acceptable methods of protest. Even celebrations turn violent as Super Bowl fans smash windows, flip and burn cars, deface property and topple light poles. World Cup victory celebrations in France took a tragic

66 SIGNS OF AN IMMINENT MASS DEPARTURE

turn after at least two citizens were killed and three children were hurt in connection with the frenzied festivities.

> **2Ti 3:1** *This know also, that <u>in the last days</u> perilous* (dangerous, furious, fierce) *times shall come.*

For the presently indifferent world or those with their heads in the clouds, this author hopes the "signs" will help cause some who are lost, confused, and "wanderers" on this earth to realize that the Word of God is true.

Jesus and His Words, not paraphrases of His Words, but His Words preserved in the English Bible (KJB), are the answer to life.

This book is not written from an academic point of view on purpose, but rather like the "Ploughman Talks" of old by the grand old preacher, Charles Spurgeon. Notice I said "like."

The Lord Jesus Christ was very blunt when He told the religious leaders of His day:

> **Mt 16:2-3** *He answered and said unto them, When it is evening, ye say, It will be fair weather: for the sky is red.* **3** *And in the morning, It will be foul weather to day: for the sky is red and lowring. O ye <u>hypocrites</u>, ye can discern the face*

> *of the sky; but can ye not discern the **signs** of the times?*

There are many hypocrites in these last of the last days. Please notice the last phrase in the following verse,

> **Heb 10:25** *Not forsaking the assembling of ourselves together, as the manner of some is; but exhorting one another: and so much the more, as ye see the day approaching.*

This is another verse that demonstrates God wants his children to be awake and aware of "signs." The two preceding verses can be summarized this way: "...can ye not discern the signs of the times...as ye see (the signs of) the day approaching"? The day is the day of judgment. I would also call your attention to the plural of "times," which indicates not just the time of Christ, but the times to come.

Perhaps, the sensational news that is reported every day has lulled many into a stupor, or else most believe there is so much "fake news," so many deceivers, so much iniquity (selfitis), so many "fake bibles," why should "I" give the future another thought. Whatever the case, attempting to discern the signs of the greatest event in human history just before it happens, is at a low point. Hopefully, reporting on 66 of these signs (six is the number of man in Scripture) will help all of us to remember:

> ***Lu 21:28*** *And <u>when these things begin to come to pass</u>, then look up, and lift up your heads; for your redemption draweth nigh.*

John Gill explained, *"then look up, and lift up your heads"* as follows:

> Be cheerful and pleasant; do not hang down your heads as bulrushes, but erect them, and put on a cheerful countenance, and look upwards, from whence your help comes; and look out wistfully and intently, for your salvation and deliverance.

Oh yes, there will be accusations about this work by some who will say: "that was taken out of context." Well, so be it, just pray the message gets across, (so, don't bother writing me) and pray, perhaps, just one will endeavor to have "clean hands," repent, believe, confess, call upon Jesus, and receive the Spirit of God.

> ***Ps 24:4-5*** *He that hath <u>clean hands</u>, and <u>a pure heart</u>; who hath not lifted up his soul unto vanity, nor sworn*

> deceitfully. **5** *He shall receive the blessing from the LORD, and righteousness from the God of his salvation.*

Why? Because this event is about to happen:

> **1Th 4:15-18** *For this we say unto you <u>by the word of the Lord</u>, that we which are alive and remain unto <u>the coming of the Lord</u> shall not prevent them which are asleep.* **16** *For <u>the Lord himself</u> shall descend from heaven with a shout, with the voice of the archangel, and with the trump of God: and the dead in Christ shall rise first:* **17** *Then we which are alive and remain shall be caught up together with them in the clouds, to meet the Lord in the air: and so shall we ever be with the Lord.* **18** *Wherefore comfort one another with these words.*

Oh yes, it may be a thousand years yet, but the "signs" indicate that we need to be watching and <u>discern the **signs** of the times</u> :

> **Mt 24:36** *But of that <u>day and hour knoweth no man</u>, no, not the angels of heaven, but my Father only.*

66 SIGNS OF AN IMMINENT MASS DEPARTURE

> ***Lu 21:36*** <u>Watch</u> *ye therefore, and pray always, that ye may be accounted worthy to escape all these things that shall come to pass, and to stand before the Son of man.*
>
> ***Mt 24:32-33*** *Now learn a parable of the fig tree; When his branch is yet tender, and putteth forth leaves, ye know that summer is nigh:* ***33*** *So likewise ye, when ye shall see all these things, know that it is near, even at the doors.*

There has been no attempt to cover "every sign." The book would be several hundred pages and contain many more signs. I wanted to keep the signs to 66, a play on the number of man and the infamous "666" of Revelation 13:18. We (my wife and I) wanted a short, inexpensive book that could easily be provided to those who need to be "yanked to attention." Some obvious additional signs that others may think important were left out. The "signs," "educational system failure" and "greed" supported by the following verses and corroborated by current test score facts and obvious greed at every level of society are two examples.

66 SIGNS OF AN IMMINENT MASS DEPARTURE

> ***2Ti 2:15*** *<u>Study</u> to shew thyself approved unto God, a workman that needeth not to be ashamed, rightly dividing the word of truth.*

> ***Mt 6:24*** *No man can serve two masters: for either he will hate the one, and love the other; or else he will hold to the one, and despise the other. Ye cannot serve God and mammon.*

I have two additional thoughts before concluding this introduction. <u>First</u>, the Bible must be interpreted literally except for obvious parables, similes, metaphors, and other "similitudes." (see *Things to Come* by Dr. Dwight Pentecost). For example, let's consider just 8 prophecies concerning the Lord Jesus Christ. Josh McDowell has documented that mathematicians such as Peter Stoner have confirmed that the probability of one person fulfilling 8 prophecies is 10 to the 17th power. That's 17 zeros. If there were 48 prophecies fulfilled it would be 157 zeros. Jesus fulfilled many more than that; some report over 400. [https://www.raptureready.com/faq-how-many-prophecies-did-jesus-fulfill/] The Lord Jesus Christ is none other than Who He said He was; God. <u>Second</u>, Pew and Gallup polls show fewer and fewer people believe the Bible is

66 SIGNS OF AN IMMINENT MASS DEPARTURE

true and that it should be 'taken' literally. Many believe the Bible is a book of fables, legends, and moral precepts recorded by man. Beliefs in reincarnation, animism, astrology, and humanism have exploded. Atheism is gaining ground. Understand that it takes faith to believe such foolishness. Why not believe the Bible, believe on Jesus, and avoid hell?

We should also mention that the formatting of one sign per page limits the available information concerning the "signs" that can be recorded in this book. There is much information on the worldwide web that is easily obtainable from search engines for each "sign." For example, information concerning the LGBTQ agenda, or drug abuse, particularly marijuana/cannabis abuse, is abundant. If a teacher or pastor decided to do a series on the "signs," he would be overwhelmed by the information readily available. There are also numerous Scripture verses that should come to mind.

Having said these things, a few, and I mean a <u>few</u> days ago, Dr. (Pastor) Steve Combs, a Director of Bearing Precious Seed Global (assists translating worldwide), author, husband, father, and a serious student of God's Words, placed the following account

66 SIGNS OF AN IMMINENT MASS DEPARTURE

on Facebook, which we have used by permission. Many good men are currently voicing the same sentiment. Something is about to happen, which we call the Rapture.

What Does the Future Hold According to the Bible?

The Bible reveals the future. It isn't a horoscope that tells you what will happen to you tomorrow (horoscopes are nearly always wrong). It reveals the future in broad outlines with some detail. The Bible includes history written in advance. I wish to summarize the path of future world history revealed in the Bible. Jesus Christ offers you the best of the future. He provided it by dying for your sins on the cross and rising physically from the dead. You must "Believe on the Lord Jesus Christ, and thou shalt be saved" (Acts 16:31)

1) The next great event on God's calendar is what we call the rapture. The word is not in the Bible, but the event is. The Lord Jesus Christ will come part way to earth and take all true Christian believers out of the world (1 Thessalonians 4:13-18; John 14:1-3). It will take place in the twinkling of an eye (1 Corinthians 15:52), but millions will be gone. Many Christians believe this will happen very soon. The dedication of a new sacrificial alter in Jerusalem in December 2018 is an indication of that.

2) A seven year protection agreement will be made between the major European leader and Israel.

3) The Jewish temple will be rebuilt and the sacrificial system restarted (Daniel 9:24-27; Revelation 11).

4) A large coalition of Muslim countries will attack Israel and God will destroy them by raining fire from heaven on them (Ezekiel 38).

5) In the middle of the seven year period, the European leader (the Antichrist) will break his agreement with Israel, march in to Jerusalem, go into the temple, sit down on the Ark of the Covenant, declare himself to be God, and demand worship (Daniel 9:27; 2 Thessalonians 2:3-4). He will make an image of himself that must be worshiped (Revelation 13). The penalty for failing to do this is death.

66 SIGNS OF AN IMMINENT MASS DEPARTURE

6) The Antichrist will control all financial transactions (Revelation 13:6-7; 14:9-11). He will become the dictator of the world.

7) God will judge the world's sin and rebellion by pouring out plagues that are worse than any event in history up to that time (Revelation 6-18). In spite of this, most will refuse to repent of their sin and turn to God.

8) Many Jews will accept Jesus Christ as their Messiah and an untold number of gentiles will receive Jesus Christ as their Savior (Revelation 7).

9) The nations of the world will gather in the valley of Megiddo in Israel for a final rebellion against God and battle against Him when He comes back. This will be the battle of Armageddon (Revelation 19).

10) At the end of the seven years of tribulation, Jesus Christ will return to earth with all the Christians (Revelation 19).

11) The Lord Jesus Christ will sit on His throne in Jerusalem and judge all from the tribulation (Matthew 25).

12) The Lord Jesus Christ will rule the earth for 1000 years (Revelation 20:1-6). All the saved people of the Old Testament and the dead of the tribulation will be resurrected.

13) The earth will be a nearly total paradise during the 1000 years. However, sin and death will still be present.

14) At the end of this 1000 year or millennial reign of Christ, there will be a final rebellion against God (Revelation 20:7-10).

15) The enemies of righteousness will once again be destroyed by fire; only, this time the entire earth and all the starry heavens will be destroyed as well (Revelation 20:9, 11; 2 Peter 3:7-10).

16) God will make a new heaven and a new earth over which He will reign forever (Revelation 21).

And I saw a new heaven and a new earth: for the first heaven and the first earth were passed away ... And God shall wipe away all tears from their eyes; and there shall be no more death, neither sorrow, nor crying, neither shall there be any more pain: for the former things are passed away. And he that sat upon the throne said, Behold, I make all things new. And he said unto me, Write: for these words are

66 SIGNS OF AN IMMINENT MASS DEPARTURE

> *true and faithful. And he said unto me, It is done. I am Alpha and Omega, the beginning and the end. I will give unto him that is athirst of the fountain of the water of life freely. (Revelation 21:1, 4-6)*

Jesus said,

> **Joh 14:15** *If ye love me, keep my commandments.*

The Holy Spirit, speaking through Paul said,

> **Heb 10:25** *Not forsaking the assembling of ourselves together, as the manner of some is; but exhorting one another: and so much the more, as ye see the day approaching.*

So few go to church in these last days that it is obvious they are either hypocrites or liars.

> **1Jo 2:4** *He that saith, I know him, and keepeth not his commandments, is a **liar**, and the truth is not in him.*

Shrug off "the dirt" of the world, repent, or rededicate your life before the shout or trumpet is heard. I believe the time for the first phase of the return of the Lord Jesus Christ is here.

> **1Th 4:16** *For the Lord himself shall descend from heaven with a shout,*

66 SIGNS OF AN IMMINENT MASS DEPARTURE

with the voice of the archangel, and with the trump of God: and the dead in Christ shall rise first:

H. D. Williams, M.D., Ph.D., President
The Old Paths Publications, Inc.
12/21/2018

SIGN #1
ARTIFICIALLY INTELLIGENT (AI) ROBOTS

Revelation 13:15 *And he had power to give life unto <u>the image of the beast, that the image of the beast should both speak,</u> and cause that as many as would not worship the image of the beast should be <u>killed</u>.*

Only an omniscient, omnipotent, omnipresent God could see the future and be able to cause the Apostle John to record these Words. The Apostle recorded that he [the Antichrist] had power to give life unto the image of the beast, that the image would speak, and cause those to be killed who would not worship the image that will be made to look like the Antichrist. Until recently, we do not know of anyone who has suggested that the "image of the beast" could be an AI robot. Who would have believed that AI robots would be developed which could look human, speak, and obey commands, even to kill.

66 SIGNS OF AN IMMINENT MASS DEPARTURE

EXAMPLES OF ROBOTIC SOLDIERS

This is an interesting video:
https://youtu.be/aRrXxqQav1w

SIGN #2

TECHNOLOGY ALLOWING THE MARK OF THE BEAST

Re 13:16 And he causeth all, both small and great, rich and poor, free and bond, to receive <u>a mark</u> in their right hand, or in their foreheads.

The subcutaneous placement of small devices, called RFID implants, that can be read by scanners, is mind-blowing. Already they are being placed for buying, selling, tracking pets, and health records.

"Last month, the FDA approved an implantable, <u>rice-grain-sized microchip</u> for use in humans. The tiny subcutaneous RFID chip, made by a company called <u>VeriChip</u>, is being marketed as a lifesaving device. If you're brought to an emergency room unconscious, a scanner in the hospital doorway will read your chip's unique ID. That will unlock your medical records from a database, allowing doctors to learn about your penicillin allergy or your pacemaker."
[Quote from: <u>https://slate.com/culture/2004/11/should-i-get-an-rfid-implant.html</u>, 12/17/2018]

Consider this:
"In a controversial move by the Catholic Church, Pope Francis has come out in vocal support of RFID Chip technologies and the extraordinary potential they hold for mankind. The outrage stems from many Evangelicals, Fundamentalists and Catholics, that RFID implants could be the "mark of the beast," as referenced in the Holy Bible."
[https://www.raptureready.com/faq-is-pope-francis-in-favor-of-the-rfid-chip/, accessed 12/2018]

66 SIGNS OF AN IMMINENT MASS DEPARTURE

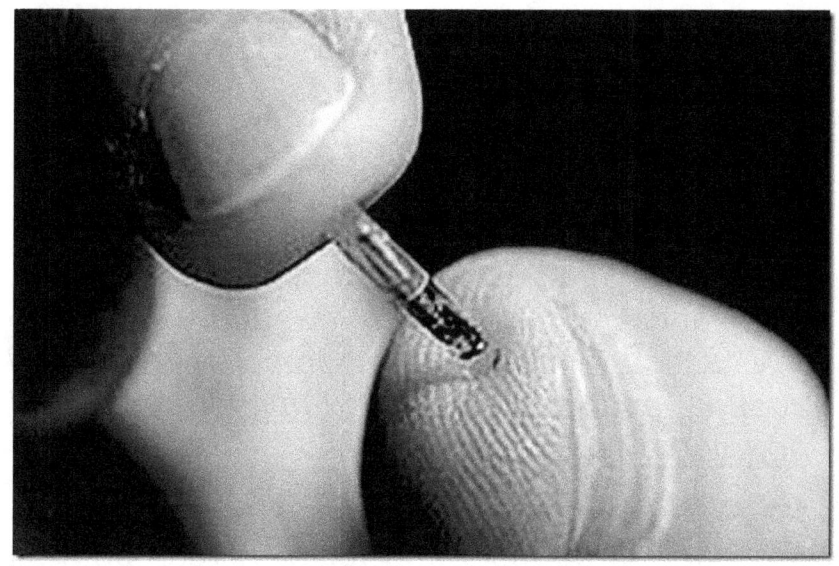

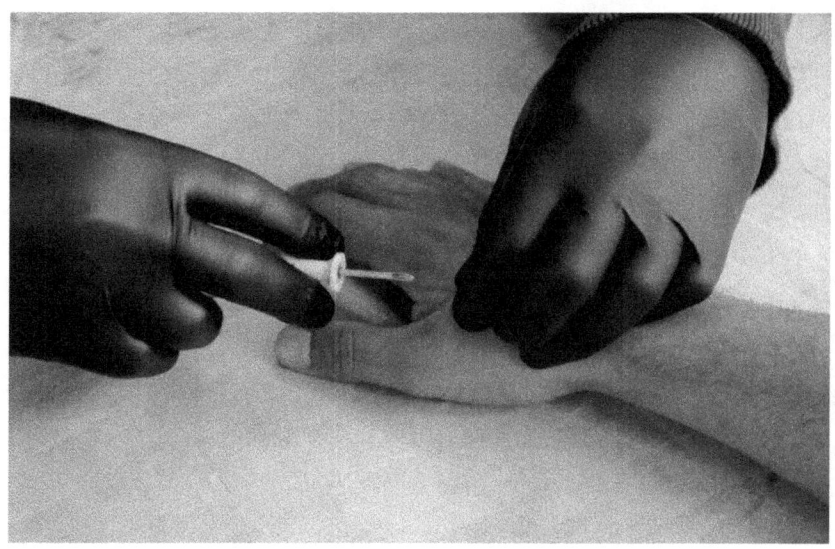

SIGN #3

GLOBAL TECHNOLOGY AND THE SPREAD OF THE GOSPEL

Ac 1:8 *But ye shall receive power, after that the Holy Ghost is come upon you: and ye shall be witnesses unto me both in Jerusalem, and in all Judaea, and in Samaria, and <u>unto the uttermost part of the earth.</u>*

Mt 24:14 *And this gospel of the kingdom shall be preached in all the world for a witness unto all nations; and then shall the end come.*

Certainly, this is taking place as we near the end of the dispensation of Grace. Many missionaries and evangelists have gone out from churches around the world. The "foolishness of preaching" has confounded the world. (And, although "few" will find the "straight" and "narrow" gate, (Mt.7:9-10) the command of Jesus to His church is already complete or soon will be.) [see Sign # 4, Global Communications and Global Travel]

SIGN #4
GLOBAL COMMUNICATIONS

Re 11:9-10 *And they of the people and kindreds and tongues and nations shall <u>see</u> their dead bodies three days and an half, and shall not suffer their dead bodies to be put in graves.* ***10*** *And they <u>that dwell upon the earth</u> shall rejoice over them, and make merry, and shall send gifts one to another; because these two prophets tormented them that dwelt on the earth.*

Re 17:8 *The beast that thou sawest was, and is not; and shall ascend out of the bottomless pit, and go into perdition: and they <u>that dwell on the earth</u> shall wonder, whose names were not written in the book of life from the foundation of the world, when they behold the beast that was, and is not, and yet is.*

These verses reveal that technological advances will allow viewers "that dwell upon the earth" to "behold" events taking place AROUND THE WORLD. The only way this could occur is by the development of the internet and the global spread of cell phones, TV, computers, radios, and other unique devices in these last days.

SIGN #5
GLOBAL CALLS FOR PEACE

1Th 5:3 *For when they shall say, <u>Peace and safety</u>; then sudden destruction cometh upon them, as travail upon a woman with child; and they shall not escape.*

Because of the tremendous unsettled turmoil around the world, many are beginning to call for a world leader to solve the problem of chaos on earth. Here is just one recent headline:

"The Whole World Is In Turmoil Not Just Us" The fierce conflicts we are witnessing in the primaries are not just an American phenomenon, indeed it's hard to find a country that isn't fighting internally as we are. Most of the world is intensely divided, and our own domestic debates are part of a global disruption.

[https://www.forbes.com/sites/michaelledeen/2016/04/01/the-whole-world-is-in-turmoil-not-just-us/, accessed 12/17/2018]

When the Global Leader (Antichrist) takes office, then many will say, "Peace and safety."

SIGN #6
GLOBAL TRAVEL

Da 12:4 But thou, O Daniel, shut up the words, and seal the book, even to the time of the end: <u>many shall run to and fro</u>, and knowledge shall be increased. Mt 28:18-20 And Jesus came and spake unto them, saying, All power is given unto me in heaven and in earth. 19 <u>Go ye therefore</u>, and teach all nations, baptizing them in the name of the Father, and of the Son, and of the Holy Ghost: 20 Teaching them to observe all things whatsoever I have commanded you: and, lo, I am with you alway, even unto the end of the world. Amen. Mr 16:15 And he said unto them, Go ye into all the world, and preach the gospel to every creature. Mt 24:14 And this gospel of the kingdom shall be preached in all the world for a witness unto all nations; and then shall the end come.

You can call today and schedule a trip to any location in the world and be there within a few hours, indicative of "shall run to and fro." We believe (rather know) Jesus would be aware of the opportunities to spread His gospel as a result of world travel capabilities, therefore His command to, "Go ye." When that is accomplished, "then shall the end come."

SIGN #7
GLOBAL PERSECUTIONS OF BELIEVERS

Mt 24:9 Then shall they deliver you up to be <u>afflicted</u>, and shall kill you: and ye shall be <u>hated</u> of all nations for my name's sake. *2Ti 3:12* Yea, and all that will live godly in Christ Jesus shall suffer <u>persecution</u>.

I continue to keep images or pictures in my mind of Islamists beheading Christians in many Muslim countries, but persecution is not limited to Islam. Now China, N. Korea,...

"Countries Where It's Hardest to Be a Christian:

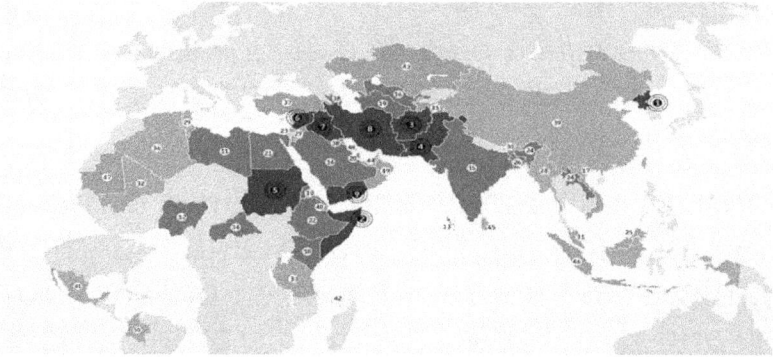

For the third year in a row, the modern persecution of Christians worldwide has hit another record high. But the primary cause, Islamic extremism, now has a rival: ethnic nationalism." [christianitytoday.com, accessed 12/2018]

SIGN #8
GLOBAL EXPLOSION IN KNOWLEDGE

Da 12:4 *But thou, O Daniel, shut up the words, and seal the book, even to the time of the end: many shall run to and fro, and <u>knowledge</u> shall be increased.*

See this graph:

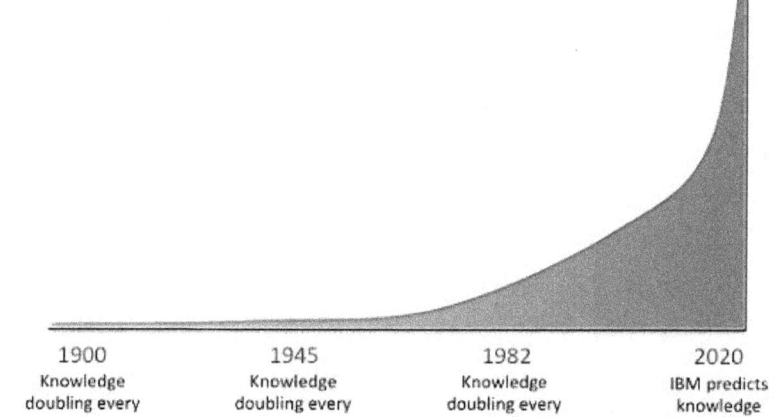

"..shocked, yet also not surprised, when I read IBM's prediction that by 2020, knowledge will likely be doubling every 11 to 12 *hours*.

[https://www.learningsolutionsmag.com/articles/2468/marc-my-words-the-coming-knowledge-tsunami accessed 12/2018]

SIGN #9
GLOBAL EXPLOSION IN SELFITIS

__2Ti 3:1-2__ This know also, that in the last days perilous times shall come. __2__ For men shall be <u>lovers of their own selves</u>, covetous, boasters, proud, blasphemers, disobedient to parents, unthankful, unholy."

The American Psychiatric Association (APA) has officially confirmed what many people thought all along: taking 'selfies' is a mental disorder. The APA made this classification during its annual board of directors meeting in Chicago. The disorder is called **selfitis**, and is defined as, "the obsessive compulsive desire to take photos of one's self and post them on social media as a way to make up for the lack of self-esteem and to fill a gap in intimacy." We have also heard of those who have accidentally killed themselves while taking "selfies."

SIGN #10
GLOBAL EXPLOSION IN IMMORALITY

2Ti 3:1,3-4 "1. This know also, that in the last days perilous times shall come 3. Without natural affection, trucebreakers, false accusers, incontinent, fierce, despisers of those that are good, 4 Traitors, heady, highminded, <u>lovers of pleasures more than lovers of God;</u>

1Th 4:3-6 For this is the will of God, even your sanctification, that ye should abstain from fornication: 4 That every one of you should know how to possess his vessel in sanctification and honour; 5 Not in the lust of concupiscence, <u>even as the Gentiles which know not God:</u> 6 That no man go beyond and defraud his brother in any matter: because that the Lord is the avenger of all such, as we also have forewarned you and testified.

Sexual immorality (sexualization and pornification) of society is seen every day on TV, in news reports, blogs, magazines, etc. Sexually transmitted diseases (STDs), many that are very resistant to treatment, have exploded (e.g., AIDS, resistant gonorrhea, hepatitis…). Just do a little research and you will be overwhelmed.

SIGN #11
GLOBAL EXPLOSION IN PORNOGRAPHY

"The amount of pornographic material available on the web is staggering. As introductory economics, search engines, and other online data repositories tell us, the market for such material is just as large. [**See 2 Tim. 3**]
Every Second:
- 28,258 users are watching pornography on the internet.
- $3,075.64 is being spent on pornography on the internet.
- 372 people are typing the word "adult" into a search engine.

Every Day:
- 37 pornographic videos are created in the United States.
- 2.5 billion emails containing porn are sent or received.
- 68 million search queries related to pornography- 25% of total searches- are generated.
- 116,000 queries related to child pornography are received.

How Online Pornography Affects Americans
- About 200,000 Americans are classified as "porn addicts."
- 40 million American people regularly visit porn sites.
- 35% of all internet downloads are related to pornography.
- 34% of internet users have experienced unwanted exposure to pornographic content through ads, pop up ads, misdirected links or emails.
- One-third of porn viewers are women."

[accessed 12/2018
https://www.webroot.com/au/en/resources/tip]

66 SIGNS OF AN IMMINENT MASS DEPARTURE

SIGN #12

GLOBAL EMERGING CHURCH

2Th 2:10-11 And with <u>all deceivableness of unrighteousness</u> in them that perish; because they received not the love of the truth, that they might be saved. 11 And for this cause God shall send them strong delusion, <u>that they should believe a lie</u>: **1Co 15:33** *Be not deceived: evil communications corrupt good manners.*

"Nothing has made me more conscious of the vicious battle that is raging for the very life and soul of Bible-believing churches than my research into the emergent church. It is frightful, because so many are falling into the devil's trap and so many more will doubtless fall in the coming days.

At the same time, it is exciting to study the emerging church, because it reminds us that the hour is very, very late and we need to be busy in the Lord's service and always "looking up."

Emerging church is the name that has been coined to define a new approach to missions and church life among some "evangelicals" that is determined more suitable for these present times."

[*What is the Emerging Church?* by David Cloud, is a must read book!]

SIGN #13

GLOBAL ABANDONMENT OF THE BIBLE

Am 8:11 Behold, the days come, saith the Lord GOD, that I will send <u>a famine</u> in the land, not a famine of bread, nor a thirst for water, but <u>of hearing the words of the LORD:</u>

This does not mean just the abandonment of the "preserved Words of God," but all books that contain the Words of God. This is the current status in nation after nation. In America, multiple surveys reveal "More than half of Americans think the Bible has too little influence on a culture they see in moral decline, yet only one in five Americans read the Bible on a regular basis, according to a new survey... If they do read it, the majority (57 percent) only read their Bibles four times a year or less. Only 26 percent of Americans said they read their Bible on a regular basis (four or more times a week)."

https://religionnews.com/2013/04/04/poll-americans-love-the-bible-but-dont-read-it-much/

Since the survey in 2013, the stats by many other surveyors demonstrate a continual decline in Bible readers.

66 SIGNS OF AN IMMINENT MASS DEPARTURE

SIGN #14

GLOBAL REWRITING OF THE BIBLE

Joh 14:21 *He that hath my commandments, and <u>keepeth</u> them, he it is that loveth me: and he that loveth me shall be loved of my Father, and I will love him, and will manifest myself to him.*

Hundreds of places in the preserved Words of God warn man about changing, adding to, or subtracting from His Words, or in other words, corrupting the Words of God. Here are two verses:

De 4:2 *Ye shall not <u>add</u> unto the word which I command you, neither shall ye <u>diminish</u> ought from it, that ye may keep the commandments of the LORD your God which I command you.*

Re 22:19 *And if any man shall <u>take away</u> from the words of the book of this prophecy, God shall take away his part out of the book of life, and out of the holy city, and from the things which are written in this book.*

Despite these warnings, many have written their own thoughts or commentary on God's Words and called them Bibles. Guilty of this are men such as Westcott and Hort, Eugene Nida, Bruce Metzger, Bart Ehrman, etc. and many organizations such as Bible Societies.

SIGN #15
THE GLOBAL OR ONE WORLD BIBLE

Re 13:1 And I stood upon the sand of the sea, and saw a beast rise up out of the sea, having seven heads and ten horns, and upon his horns ten crowns, and upon his heads the name of blasphemy. Da 7:23 Thus he said, The fourth beast shall be <u>the fourth kingdom upon earth, which shall be diverse from all kingdoms, and shall devour the whole earth, and shall tread it down, and break it in pieces.</u>

At the end of this age, extensive alterations of the Bible are occurring for the "New World Order," the antichrist, and the false prophet. These new perversions satisfy the LGBTQ crowd, Chrislam believers, the gender neutral advocates, and marriage-denying supporters. Separate "bibles" are already in existence which support these doctrines, but all that is needed is to combine all of the corruption into one all-inclusive book and call it a "bible." As a publisher, I can report that it would only take about a month to publish such a volume. Some examples are: The recently released "Queen James Bible" available on Amazon and the Chrislam Bibles, amalgamating Islam and Christianity published a few years ago, but greatly denied. Rick Warren is heavily involved in activities supporting Chrislam.

SIGN #16
GLOBAL APOSTASY

2Th 2:2-3 That ye be not soon shaken in mind, or be troubled, neither by spirit, nor by word, nor by letter as from us, as that the day of Christ is at hand. 3 Let no man deceive you by any means: for that day shall not come, except there come <u>a falling away first,</u> and that man of sin be revealed, the son of perdition;

Many have noted that the Greek Word behind "a falling away" above is "*apostasía*," which means a forsaking of or defection from truth. Societies are not only devouring "fake" news, but are experiencing defection from Christian doctrine, from virtue (moral purity), and from faith in God's Son, which God continually commands throughout His Bible. Christianity is now rejected and even demonized, characterized by a complete renunciation of the clear and pure commandments of a Holy God. "Paul, Jude, and Peter all foresaw an immense surge in religious leaders and their followers "falling away" from the truth in the last days. The ultimate expression of that is in the Antichrist himself."

[http://www.dtbm.org/sermon/global-apostasy/ accessed 12/18/2018]

SIGN #17

THE GLOBAL LEADER (Antichrist)

Re 13:8 And all that dwell upon the earth <u>shall worship him</u>, (Antichrist) whose names are not written in the book of life of the Lamb slain from the foundation of the world. [See all of Rev. 13, and Daniel]

2Th 2:3 3 Let no man deceive you by any means: for that day shall not come, except there come <u>a falling away first,</u> and that <u>man of sin</u> be revealed, the <u>son of perdition</u>;

Many, many verses in the Bible reveal the character and disposition of the Antichrist. The name "antichrist" is only found in 1 John 2:18, 2:22, 4:3, and 2 John 7. The Apostle John was the only Bible writer to use the name antichrist. Studying these verses, we learn that many antichrists (false teachers) will appear between the time of Christ's first and second coming, but there will be one great antichrist who will rise to power during the end times, or "last time," as 1 John phrases it (1 John 2:18). The antichrist will deny that Jesus is the Christ. He will deny both God the Father and God the Son, and will be a liar and a deceiver. [<u>See the books of Daniel and Thessalonians</u>.]

SIGN #18
GLOBAL PESTILENCES

Mt 24:7 For nation shall rise against nation, and kingdom against kingdom: and there shall be famines, and <u>pestilences,</u> and earthquakes, in divers places.

"Up to 319 people dead as Congo Ebola outbreak worsens"
[https://www.cnn.com/2018/12/18/health/ebola-democratic-republic-of-congo-intl/index.html, accessed 12/2018]

"New diseases emerge all the time, and sexually transmitted infections, also known as sexually transmitted diseases, are no exception. Here are four bacteria that could become serious public health threats. (Warning: contains a description of animal auto-fellatio.)" On the following page are warnings about 4 STDs.
[https://www.cnn.com/2018/12/06/health/std-sexually-transmitted-diseases-partner/, accessed 12/2018]

There are numerous "plagues" or "pestilences" currently sweeping the world such as Ebola, AIDS, AFP (Acute Flaccid Paralysis), and many drug resistant sexually transmitted diseases.

SIGN #19
THE GLOBAL GOVERNMENT

*Re 13:13-17 And he doeth great wonders, so that he maketh fire come down from heaven on the earth in the sight of men, **14** And deceiveth them that <u>dwell on the earth</u> by the means of those miracles which he had power to do in the sight of the beast; saying to them that dwell on the earth, that they should make an image to the beast, which had the wound by a sword, and did live. **15** And he had power to give life unto the image of the beast, that the image of the beast should both speak, and cause that as many as would not worship the image of the beast should be killed. **16** And he causeth <u>all</u>, both small and great, rich and poor, free and bond, to receive a mark in their right hand, or in their foreheads: **17** And that no man might buy or sell, save he that had the mark, or the name of the beast, or the number of his name.*

The recent death of former President George W. Bush reminds us of his statement calling for a one world government: He said: "We have before us the opportunity to forge for ourselves and for future generation a new world order." "One World Government Quotes By World Leaders: Henry Kissinger, David Rockefeller, Al Gore, Barack Hussein Obama, French President Chirac, Strobe Talbott, Mikhail Gorbachev, Robert Kennedy, UK Prime Minister Gordon Brown, Nelson Mandela, George McGovern, Robert Mueller."
[http://www.arewelivinginthelastdays.com/com/quotes.html accessed 12/2018]

SIGN #20
THE GLOBAL REGATHERING OF ISRAEL

Hab 1:5 Behold ye among the heathen, and regard, and wonder marvellously: for <u>I will work a work in your days, which ye will not believe,</u> though it be told you. **Jer 16:14-15** *Therefore, behold, the days come, saith the LORD, that it shall no more be said, The LORD liveth, that brought up the children of Israel out of the land of Egypt; 15 But, The LORD liveth, that brought up the children of Israel from the land of the north, and from all the lands <u>whither he had driven them: and I will bring them again into their land that I gave unto their fathers</u>.* **Isa 11:10-12** *And in that day there shall be a root of Jesse, which shall stand for an ensign of the people; to it shall the Gentiles seek: and his rest shall be glorious. 11 And it shall come to pass in that day, that the Lord shall set his hand again the second time <u>to recover the remnant of his people</u>, which shall be left, from Assyria, and from Egypt, and from Pathros, and from Cush, and from Elam, and from Shinar, and from Hamath, and from the islands of the sea. 12 And he shall set up an ensign for the nations, and shall <u>assemble the outcasts of Israel, and gather together the dispersed of Judah from the four corners of the earth.</u>* [I do not need to comment, there are many many verses heralding this event]

SIGN #21
THE GLOBALLY OCCURRING EARTHQUAKES

Mt 24:7 For nation shall rise against nation, and kingdom against kingdom: and there shall be famines, and pestilences, and <u>earthquakes</u>, in <u>divers</u> places.

Many geologists are proclaiming that the number of earthquakes around the world is or will be accelerating. On this day, 12/18/2018,

- 187 earthquakes in the past 24 hours
- 1,494 earthquakes in the past 7 days
- 7,380 earthquakes in the past 30 days
- 88,863 earthquakes in the past 365 days

"Scientists have warned there could be a big increase in numbers of devastating earthquakes around the world next year. They believe variations in the speed of Earth's rotation could trigger intense seismic activity, particularly in heavily populated tropical regions."

[https://www.theguardian.com/world/2017/nov/18/2018-set-to-be-year-of-big-earthquakes, accessed 12/2018]

It appears something is happening: "Quakes are increasing, but scientists aren't sure what it means."

[https://www.latimes.com/local/la-me-la-quakes-20140603-story.html accessed 12/2018]

SIGN #22
THE GLOBAL LAWLESSNESS

Mt 24:12 And because iniquity shall abound, the love of many shall wax cold.

The lawlessness (= iniquity = anomia) sweeping the world is unprecedented. Just do a brief search:

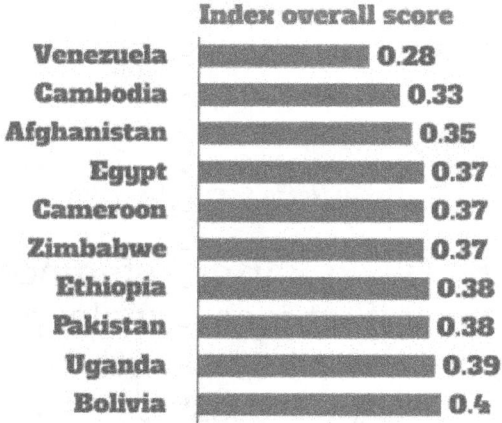

The ten most lawless countries

Country	Index overall score
Venezuela	0.28
Cambodia	0.33
Afghanistan	0.35
Egypt	0.37
Cameroon	0.37
Zimbabwe	0.37
Ethiopia	0.38
Pakistan	0.38
Uganda	0.39
Bolivia	0.4

In chapter 24 of Matthew, Jesus discusses the "signs" of the end. In the verse above, Jesus relates that "iniquity shall abound." Iniquity comes from a word, *anomia*, meaning lawlessness. In the USA, the Department of Justice graphs show a horrible, significant rise in lawlessness. See the next page.

66 SIGNS OF AN IMMINENT MASS DEPARTURE

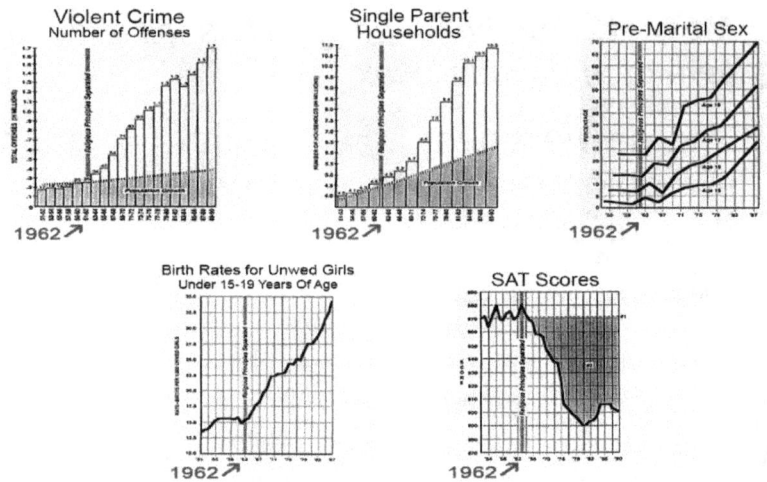

(Source) America: To Pray or Not to Pray by David Barton
ISBN-13: 978-0925279422 • ISBN-10: 0925279420

These charts by David Barton reference the increase in "violent crimes, single parent households, pre-marital sex, birth rates of unwed girls, and SAT scores" since prayer was removed from schools in 1962. In my book "The Lie That Changed the Modern World," I placed numerous graphs obtained from the Department of Justice depicting incarcerations, violent crimes, and death row inmates, and related them to the introduction of 'new' bible versions from the '50s until the '70s. The graphs look just like these above.

66 SIGNS OF AN IMMINENT MASS DEPARTURE

SIGN #23

GLOBALLY DROUGHTS & FAMINE INCREASING

Mt 24:7 For nation shall rise against nation, and kingdom against kingdom: and there shall be famines, and pestilences, and earthquakes, in divers places. **Re 18:8** *Therefore shall her [Babylon] plagues come in one day, death, and mourning, and famine; and she shall be utterly burned with fire: for strong is the Lord God who judgeth her.*

The UN said 900 million people were hungry last year. Many are reporting that deserts are expanding. This phenomenon is called "desertification." The reasons given are unplanned agriculture, overgrazing, excessive firewood collection, industrialization, and other human factors. Whatever the cause, the Lord Jesus Christ gave this as a "sign" that the end is near or coming. Famine is often a result of droughts produced by "desertification."
[http://earthuntouched.com/deserts-expanding/ accessed 12/2018]

Consider this one country: "We work in Zambia, a country in Africa that has among the highest rates of nutrition problems in the world. 40% of kids there suffer from stunting —low growth due to malnutrition over time."

SIGN #24
GLOBAL FALSE PROPHET(S)

Mt 24:11 And <u>many false prophets</u> shall rise, and shall deceive many. ***Re 13:11-12** And I beheld another beast coming up out of the earth; and he had two horns like a lamb, and he spake as a dragon. **12** And he exerciseth all the power of the first beast before him, and causeth the earth and them which dwell therein to worship the first beast, whose deadly wound was healed. **13** And he doeth…wonders.*

The world is being prepared by the numerous false Christian leaders abounding in the world, and the One World Bible being generated to accept the <u>"false prophet"</u> who will assist the Antichrist. I suggest that you search "false pastors" on the worldwide web. You will marvel at what comes up. One well-known person is Benny Hinn. He "was a disciple of the infamous false teacher, Kathryn Khulman, and he propagates the false doctrines that she taught. He has adopted other false teachings from Kenny Copeland and Ken Hagin who picked up the heretical Mormon doctrine that all men can become a god. Benny also teaches the heretical doctrine that YAHSHUA [meaning Jesus] was born-again in Hell. He is a leading "word faith" false teacher who is not born from above and headed straight to Hell! dov-hinn.html" [http://freeworldfilmworks.com/dov-10danger.htm accessed 12/2018][my addition: Jesus from Yeshua]

SIGN #25
GLOBAL NUCLEAR DISASTER

Mt 24:22 And except those days should be shortened, there should no flesh be saved: but for the elect's sake those days shall be shortened. [See Mk. 13:20]

Most people dwelling on the earth are totally unaware of the "extinction level event" (ELE) that occurred in Japan: the Fukushima nuclear power plant meltdown as a result of the severe 6.6 M earthquake experienced 4/11/2011. Many reports on the internet are saying: "BUT THEN THERE'S FUKUSHIMA...WHAT MANY ARE CALLING AN "EXTINCTION LEVEL EVENT" BECAUSE NO ONE AND NOTHING PRESENTLY KNOWN CAN STOP THE RELEASE OF TOXIC RADIATION FROM THAT PLANT!" Deadly radiation is pouring into the ocean and atmospheric winds are carrying rads everywhere.
[https://www.infowars.com/fukushima-is-falling-apart-are-you-ready-for-a-mass-extinction-event/ accessed 12/2018]

What follows are pictures of sea life affected by Fukushima radiation as well as a map showing the spread of radiation.

Re 8:8-9 And the second angel sounded, and as it were a great mountain burning with fire was cast into the sea: and the third part of the sea became blood; 9 And the third part of the creatures which were in the sea, and had life, died; and the third part of the ships were destroyed.

66 SIGNS OF AN IMMINENT MASS DEPARTURE

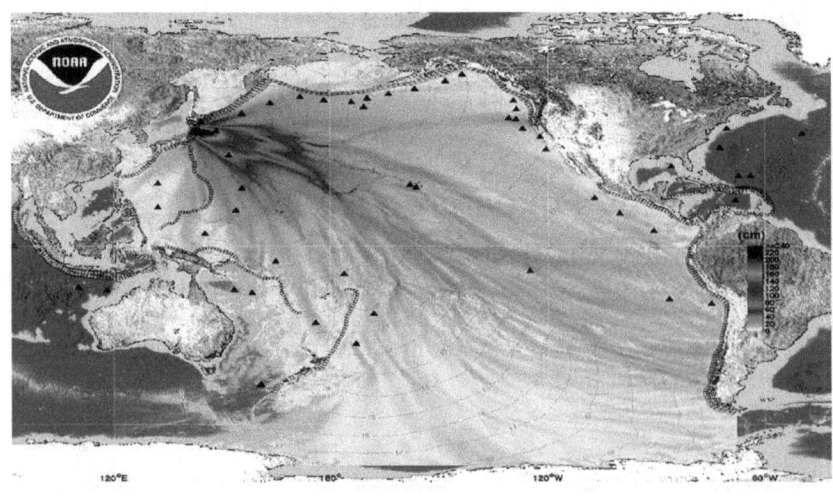

SIGN #26
GLOBALLY LOVE WAXING COLD

Mt 24:10, 12 And then shall many be offended, and shall betray one another, and shall <u>hate</u> one another. 12 And because iniquity shall abound, the <u>love of many shall wax cold</u>.

Can anyone deny this proclamation by the Lord Jesus Christ as a "sign" of the end? Just consider worldwide stats about murder, deceit, fornication, adultery, pedophilia, rape, crime, homosexuality, gender problems, decreased church attendance, child abuse, and betrayal of friends. Most sanctified, God-loving, God-honouring men believe these are the reasons: the love of the world, which has a ruler, named Satan, and the yielding to the flesh:

1Jo 2:15 Love not the world, neither the things that are in the world. If any man love the world, the love of the Father is not in him. 1Jo 2:16 For all that is in the world, the lust of the flesh, and the lust of the eyes, and the pride of life, is not of the Father, but is of the world. Joh 12:31 Now is the judgment of this world: now shall the prince of this world be cast out. Eph 2:2 Wherein in time past ye walked according to the course of this world, according to the prince of the power of the air, the spirit that now worketh in the children of disobedience:

SIGN #27
GLOBAL DECLINE OF THE WEST

***2Th 3:10** For even when we were with you, this we commanded you, that if any would not work, neither should he eat.*

The pressure placed on western civilization by "Cultural Marxism," "socialism," "communism," or whatever you want to call it, is wreaking havoc in nations, including America. Some code words are: "progressivism" or "social justice," or "redistribution of wealth," or "materialist rationalism." The proof of the pudding is observing the results of socialism in countries such as Venezuela, Russia, and China. It doesn't work.

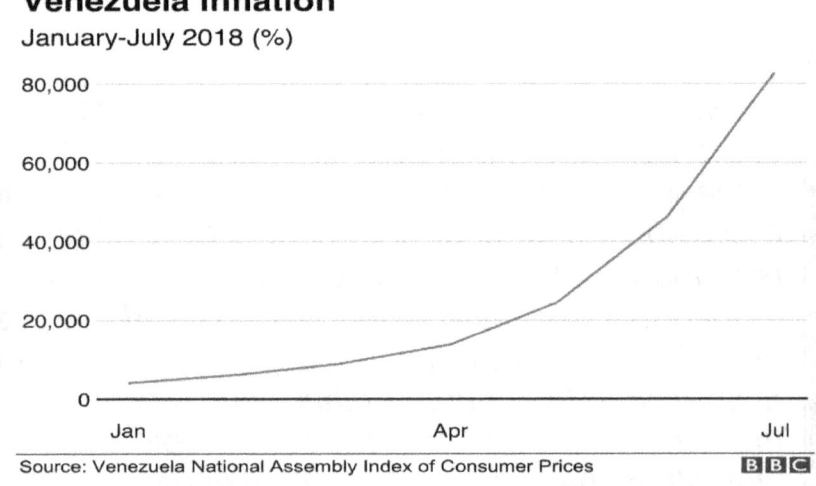

Venezuela inflation
January-July 2018 (%)

Source: Venezuela National Assembly Index of Consumer Prices — BBC

SIGN #28
GLOBAL UNUSUAL WEATHER

Isa 24:4-6 The earth mourneth and fadeth away, the world languisheth and fadeth away, the haughty people of the earth do languish. 5 The earth also is defiled under the inhabitants thereof; because they have transgressed the laws, changed the ordinance, broken the everlasting covenant. 6 Therefore hath the curse devoured the earth, and they that dwell therein are desolate: therefore the inhabitants of the earth are burned, and few men left. Lu 21:25 And there shall be signs in the sun, and in the moon, and in the stars; and upon the earth distress of nations, with perplexity; the sea and the waves roaring; Eze 38:22 And I will plead against him with pestilence and with blood; and I will rain upon him, and upon his bands, and upon the many people that are with him, an overflowing rain, and great hailstones, fire, and brimstone. Job 38:22-23 Hast thou entered into the treasures of the snow? or hast thou seen the treasures of the hail, 23 Which I have reserved against the time of trouble, against the day of battle and war?

News accounts about these phenomena are abundant worldwide.

SIGN #29
GLOBAL SPIRITUAL BLINDNESS

Mt 24:37-38 But as the <u>days of Noe were</u>, so shall also the coming of the Son of man be. 38 For as in the days that were before the flood they were eating and drinking, marrying and giving in marriage, until the day that Noe entered into the ark. Mt 23:24 Ye <u>blind guides</u>, which strain at a gnat, and swallow a camel.

In the Bible, we find frequent expressions such as "the last days," "the end times," the "day of Christ," "the day of God," which all have different meanings, but all refer to future prophetic signs and events. In the passage above, Jesus indicates that most people will be totally oblivious to the signs. I believe that during the tribulation, the blindness will continue until the second phase of the second coming of the Lord when he plants His feet on the Mount of Olives. One would think the rapture would wake up many, but we know it will probably be explained away because Jesus said, "*Luke 18:8 ...Nevertheless when the Son of man cometh, shall he find faith on the earth?*" There will not be many missing from the earth because most do not believe the Bible, the "Final Authority." And if you do not believe its testimony about Jesus Christ, you will be left behind.

SIGN #30
BLINDNESS OF ISRAEL

Ro 2:17 Behold, thou art called a Jew, and restest in the law, and makest thy boast of God, Ro 2:19 And art confident that thou thyself art a <u>guide of the blind</u>, a light of them which are in darkness, Ro 11:25 For I would not, brethren, that ye should be ignorant of this mystery, lest ye should be wise in your own conceits; that <u>blindness</u> in part is happened to Israel, until the fulness of the Gentiles be come in.

I will never forget Dr. Dwight Pentecost reporting that a high-ranking officer in Israel's Defense Force (IDF) asked him how he knew that Israel would defeat the Arab nation forces in the 1967 Arab-Israeli War. Dr. Pentecost explained from the Bible but he said that "as the officer left, he proclaimed, "God had nothing to do with Israel winning." This demonstrates dramatically the "blindness" of Israel. The Apostle Paul explained it this way: "*Ro 9:31-32 But Israel, which followed after the law of righteousness, hath not attained to the law of righteousness. 32 Wherefore? Because they sought it not by faith, but as it were by the works of the law. For they stumbled at that stumblingstone;*" [who is Jesus Christ]

66 SIGNS OF AN IMMINENT MASS DEPARTURE

SIGN #31
ISRAEL DECLARED A NATION

***Isa 66:8** Who hath heard such a thing? who hath seen such things? Shall the earth be made to bring forth in one day? or shall a <u>nation</u> be born at once? for as soon as Zion travailed, she brought forth her children. Ro 11:26 And so all Israel shall be saved: as it is written, There shall come out of Sion the Deliverer, and shall turn away ungodliness from Jacob:*

"The Balfour Declaration ("Balfour's promise" in Arabic) was a public pledge by Britain in 1917 declaring its aim to establish "a national home for the Jewish people" in Palestine. The statement came in the form of a letter from Britain's then-foreign secretary, Arthur Balfour, addressed to Lionel Walter Rothschild, a figurehead of the British Jewish community. It was made during World War I (1914-1918) and was included in the terms of the British Mandate for Palestine after the dissolution of the Ottoman empire...Upon the start of the mandate, the British began to facilitate the immigration of European Jews to Palestine. Between 1922 and 1935, the Jewish population rose from nine percent to nearly 27 percent of the total population."

"Israel became a nation on **May 14, 1948**, after it was recognized as a country in the Middle East by the United Nations. This caused Arab nations, such as Egypt, Iraq, Lebanon and Syria to attack Israel on the same day it gained independence."

The "bones" in Eze. 37:3-6 typify this entire account:

***Eze 37:5-6** Thus saith the Lord GOD unto these bones; Behold, I will cause breath to enter into you, and ye shall live: **6** And I will lay sinews upon you, and will bring up flesh upon you, and cover you with skin, and put breath in you, and ye shall live; and ye shall know that I am the LORD.*

SIGN #32

ISRAEL SUPERNATURALLY PROTECTED

Ge 12:3 And I will bless them that bless thee, and <u>curse him that curseth thee</u>: and in thee shall all families of the earth be blessed.

Zec 12:8-9 In that day shall the LORD <u>defend</u> the inhabitants of Jerusalem; and he that is feeble among them at that day shall be as David; and the house of David shall be as God, as the angel of the LORD before them. 9 And it shall come to pass in that day, that I will seek to destroy all the nations that come against Jerusalem.

"There are hundreds of stories of how God has preserved and miraculously protected the Jewish nation and people. As End-Times prophecy states, God still has a purpose for His Jewish nation, and He will bring it to pass. Satan has tried to rid of the Jews throughout history, and Satan's Anti-Christ is trying to split Jerusalem, but God will intervene. The Jewish people will realize that the Anti-Christ is a fake Messiah, and will realize they had crucified the real Messiah, Jesus Christ. When the Jewish nation calls out to their Messiah, then Jesus' Second-Coming will be fulfilled. You, the believers, the Church, will come with Him, on that glorious day at Armageddon"

[https://armageddonapocalypse.wordpress.com/2010/04/14/israel-protected-miraculously-by-god-to-fulfill-end-times-prophecy/ ACCESSED 12/2018]

Some accounts are found here: "Israel Protected Miraculously By God To Fulfill End-Times Prophecy."

SIGN #33

ISRAEL AND ANTISEMITISM

De 28:37 And thou shalt become <u>an astonishment</u>, a proverb, and <u>a byword, among all nations</u> whither the LORD shall lead thee.

Jer 29:18 And I will <u>persecute them</u> with the sword, with the famine, and with the pestilence, and will deliver them to be removed to all the kingdoms of the earth, to be a curse, and an astonishment, and an hissing, and <u>a reproach</u>, among all the nations whither I have driven them:

Germany's attempt to annihilate the Jews in WWII under Hitler during the Holocaust is just one example of the extreme antisemitism prevalent in the world. Recently, its ugliness has arisen again in Russia, Germany, France, Britain, Egypt, USA (by attacks on Synagogues and swastikas painted in many places), and many other nations. Antisemitism also goes by the name, "anti-Zionism," and is called "new antisemitism," (Wikipedia) but it is not 'new.'

"Until recent years, many Jews in America believed that the worst of anti-Semitism was over there, in Europe, a vestige of the old country...So the **massacre on Saturday of 11 people in a Pittsburgh synagogue,** by a man who told the police when he surrendered that he "wanted all Jews to die," was for many a shocking wake-up call." [Article in the New York Times, Oct. 29, 2018]

SIGN #34
ISRAEL'S CAPITAL IS AGAIN JERUSALEM

Ps 137:5 If I forget thee, O Jerusalem, let my right hand forget her cunning. **Zec 8:3** *Thus saith the LORD; I am returned unto Zion, and will dwell in the midst of Jerusalem: and Jerusalem shall be called a city of truth; and the mountain of the LORD of hosts the holy mountain.* **Zec 14:2** *For I will gather all nations against Jerusalem to battle; and the city shall be taken, and the houses rifled, and the women ravished; and half of the city shall go forth into captivity, and the residue of the people shall not be cut off from the city.*

"On December 6, 2017, US President Donald Trump announced the United States recognition of Jerusalem as the capital of Israel and ordered the planning of the relocation of the U.S. Embassy in Israel from Tel Aviv to Jerusalem. Benjamin Netanyahu, the Prime Minister of Israel, welcomed the decision and praised the announcement." (Wikipedia)

"This is a major move for the U.S. and a significant event relative to End Times prophecy. The Bible clearly places Israel back in their land and in control of Jerusalem before the major events of the Last Days occur." [https://endtimestruth.com/trump-to-recognize-jerusalem-as-israels-capital/ accessed 12/2018]

Zechariah 14:2 clearly indicates Jerusalem will be attacked when Armageddon occurs and one of the reasons is the declaration of it as Israel's capital again. It is "the cup of trembling." Isa 51:17, 22, Zec. 12:2

66 SIGNS OF AN IMMINENT MASS DEPARTURE

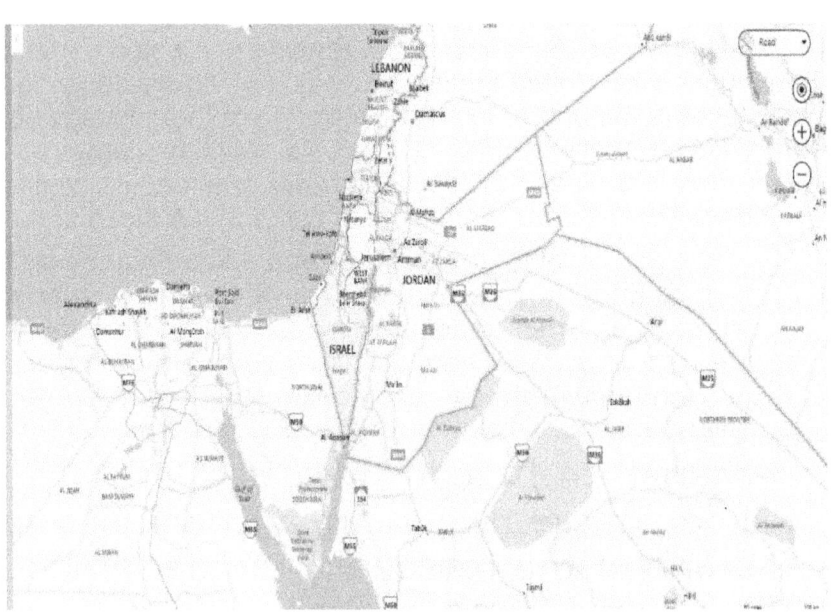

SIGN #35
ISRAEL'S 3rd TEMPLE

Eze 40:4 And the man said unto me, Son of man, behold with thine eyes, and hear with thine ears, and set thine heart upon all that I shall shew thee; for to the intent that I might shew them unto thee art thou brought hither: <u>declare all that thou seest to the house of Israel. [See chapters 40-48]</u> Re 11:1 And there was given me a reed like unto a rod: and the angel stood, saying, Rise, and measure <u>the temple of God,</u> and the altar, and them that worship therein.

Dr. David Cloud reported on 12/7/2018: "The preparation for the building of the Third Temple [in Israel] is reaching <u>fever pitch</u>."

From recent discoveries, it appears that the Temple mount is located "<u>down</u>" a short incline from where the current Dome of the Rock is located. The "Dome" stands upon the former Fortress of Antonia as Scripture indicates: *Ac 21:32 Who immediately took soldiers and centurions, and ran <u>down</u> unto them: and when they saw the chief captain and the soldiers, they left beating of Paul.*

66 SIGNS OF AN IMMINENT MASS DEPARTURE

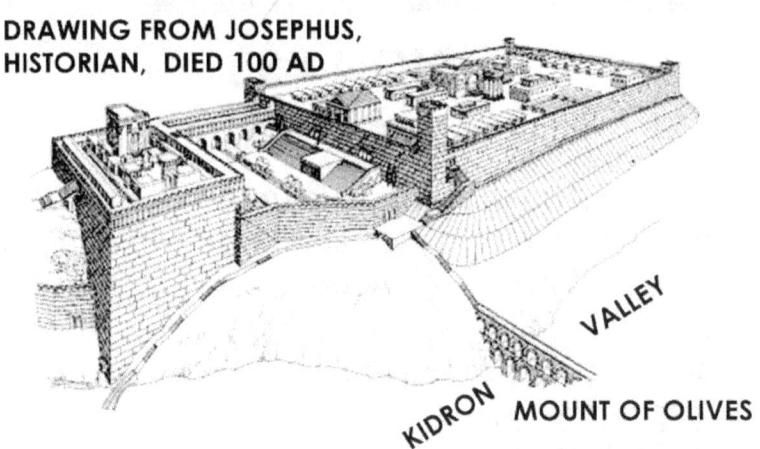

SIGN #36

IMPLEMENTS HAVE BEEN MADE FOR THE 3rd TEMPLE

Ex 25:9 *According to all that I shew thee, after the <u>pattern of the tabernacle</u>, and the pattern of all the <u>instruments</u> thereof, even so shall ye make it.* *Ex 25:40* *And look that thou make them after their <u>pattern</u>, which was shewed thee in the <u>mount.</u>*

Re 11:1 *And there was given me a reed like unto a rod: and the angel stood, saying, Rise, and measure <u>the temple of God</u>, and the altar, and them that worship therein.*

Most know the tabernacle in the wilderness (Moses' tabernacle) was patterned after the Temple in Heaven as God instructed Moses when he was on the "mount. The Temple Institute in Israel said:

"We are pleased to announce that the weaving of the sacred Ephod garment for the uniform of the High Priest has been completed. The Temple Institute has also completed the complicated task of joining the ephod to the remembrance stones, and affixing the breastplate. This complex project has been based on extensive research by the Institute. With G-d's help this task has been completed and the results have been made public."

On the webpage link below are links to the <u>instruments</u> and <u>their descriptions.</u> We have placed a few pictures on the pages to follow

[https://www.templeinstitute.org/vessels_gallery_16.htm accessed 12/2018]

66 SIGNS OF AN IMMINENT MASS DEPARTURE

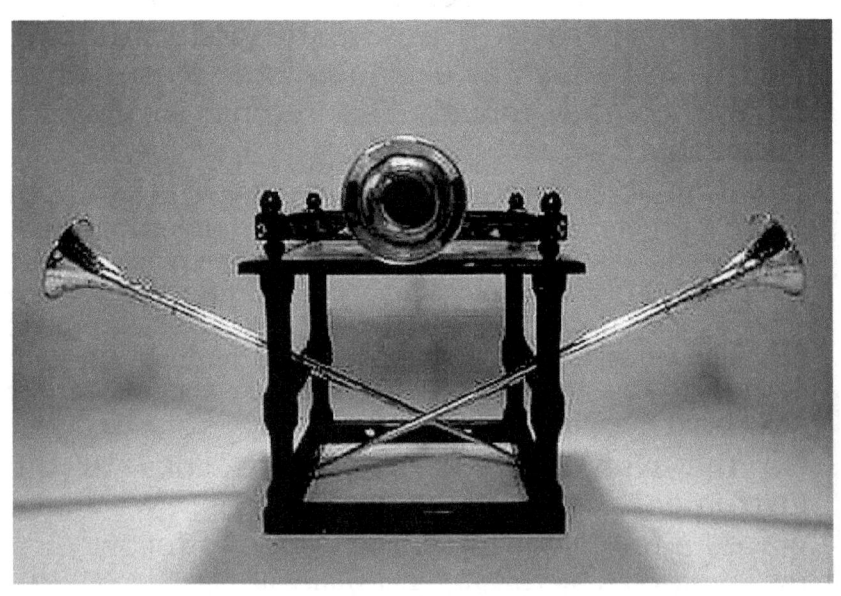

66 SIGNS OF AN IMMINENT MASS DEPARTURE

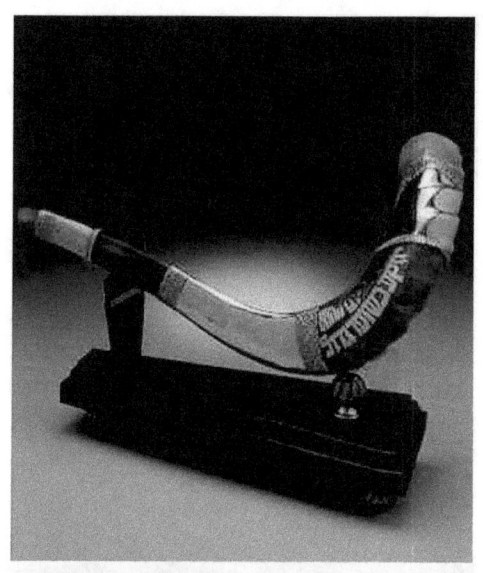

66 SIGNS OF AN IMMINENT MASS DEPARTURE

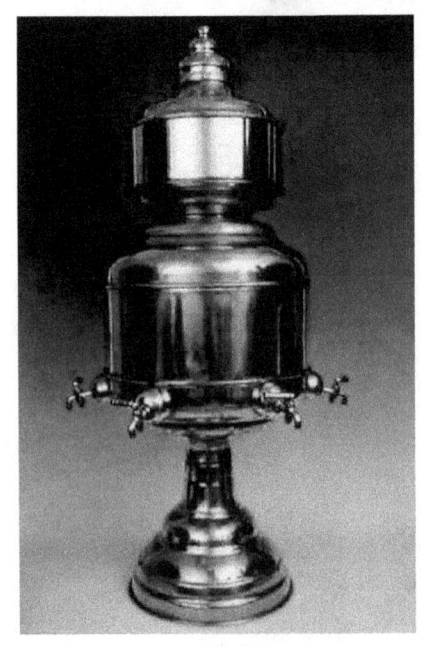

66 SIGNS OF AN IMMINENT MASS DEPARTURE

66 SIGNS OF AN IMMINENT MASS DEPARTURE

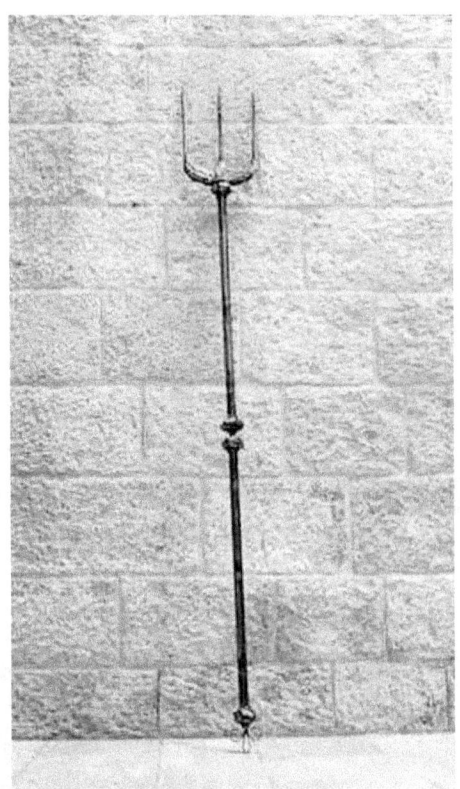

66 SIGNS OF AN IMMINENT MASS DEPARTURE

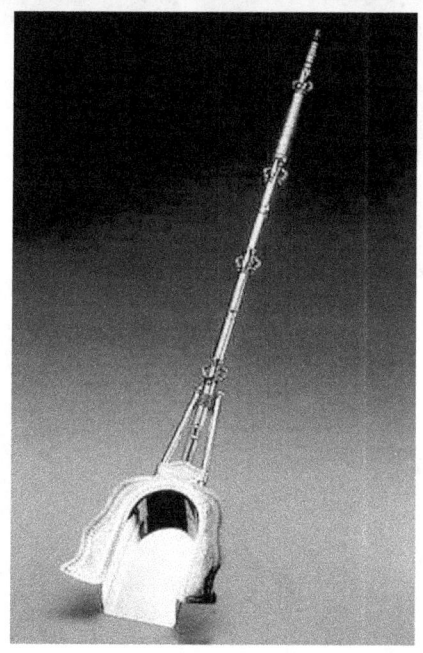

66 SIGNS OF AN IMMINENT MASS DEPARTURE

66 SIGNS OF AN IMMINENT MASS DEPARTURE

66 SIGNS OF AN IMMINENT MASS DEPARTURE

SIGN #37

ISRAEL'S DEDICATION OF THE ALTAR FOR THE 3rd TEMPLE

Ex 20:24-25 An <u>altar</u> of earth thou shalt make unto me, and shalt sacrifice thereon thy burnt offerings, and thy peace offerings, thy sheep, and thine oxen: in all places where I record my name I will come unto thee, and I will bless thee. 25 And if thou wilt <u>make me an altar</u> of stone, thou shalt not build it of hewn stone: for if thou lift up thy tool upon it, thou hast polluted it.

Dr. David Cloud reported "On December 10, 2018 the last evening of Hanukkah, the "nascent" Jewish Sanhedrin consecrated a stone sacrificial altar."

According to Adam Eliyahu Berkowitz' report in Breaking Israel News the altar has been prepared with stones made of aerated concrete and "fit for use in the Temple." The current stones are in loose form ready to be moved to the Temple Mount and stored so they would be available "at a moment's notice," but there also are plans to re-create the pieces from actual stones, considered the "ideal material from which to build the altar." [Read more at https://www.wnd.com/2018/12/nations-invited-to-consecration-of-altar-for-3rd-temple/, accessed 12/2018]

The preparations for the 3rd temple are at a "fever pitch." It will be built where the Al Aqsa Mosque is located, recent discoveries show, not where the Dome of the Rock situated.

66 SIGNS OF AN IMMINENT MASS DEPARTURE

SIGN #38

THE EASTERN GATE IS SHUT UNTIL...

Eze 44:1-3 Then he brought me back the way of the gate of the outward sanctuary which looketh toward <u>the east</u>; and <u>it was shut</u>. 2 Then said the LORD unto me; <u>This gate shall be shut</u>, it shall not be opened, and no man shall enter in by it; because the LORD, the God of Israel, hath entered in by it, therefore it shall be shut. 3 It is for the prince; the prince, he shall sit in it to eat bread before the LORD; he shall enter by the way of the porch of that gate, and shall go out by the way of the same.

SIGN #39

OFFERINGS BEGINNING FOR THE 3rd TEMPLE

Mal 3:4 Then shall the <u>offering</u> of Judah and Jerusalem be pleasant unto the LORD, <u>as in the days of old, and as in former years</u>.

"The Jewish Council (Sanhedrin) is planning to consecrate a stone sacrificial altar and perform the daily offering that occurred every morning and evening in the ancient temple. The sacrifice will be enacted by Kohanim (Levites) dressed in biblical priestly attire. It is not known whether the lamb will be sacrificed at the site, but meat will be roasted on the altar. Rabbi Yoel Schwartz states, "We are very close to the time about which the prophets of Israel prophesied that the God of the world who created everything will be called by the world in the name of the God of Israel, for only the people of Israel remained attached to Him.... God's call to return his people to his land will show that the belief of some nations that Israel was in exile as a punishment was a mistaken belief. The exile was only for Israel to serve as an example to the nations for serving God. ... Now, it is time for the Creator's people to return to their land, and from here light will come forth to the world. And when we merit it, and the Temple will be restored and built on its place, then even more will all the nations realize that the time has come to worship God"

SIGN #40

ISRAEL IS BOOMING, BLOOMING, & PROSPERING

***Isa 35:1-2** The wilderness and the solitary place shall be glad for them; and the desert shall rejoice, and <u>blossom</u> as the rose. **2** It shall <u>blossom</u> abundantly, and rejoice even with joy and singing: the glory of Lebanon shall be given unto it, the excellency of Carmel and Sharon, they shall see the glory of the LORD, and the excellency of our God. **Isa 41:18** I will open rivers in high places, and fountains in the midst of the valleys: <u>I will make the wilderness a pool of water, and the dry land springs of water.</u>*

As I was beginning this "sign," an article came in from Dr. D. Cloud, Way of Life Literature concerning this very thing: "The Land of Israel in 1867." The import of the entire article is the desolation of the land under the rule of Islamists as verified by Mark Twain. Now, many news reports reveal Israel has developed the land using new technology and the deserts are blooming and springs are bubbling out of the ground, just as Scripture indicates.
[https://www1.cbn.com/cbnnews/israel/2018/june/israelis-use-technology-to-make-the-desert-bloom, accessed 12/2018] and

https://www.dailymail.co.uk/sciencetech/article-2582777/The-incredible-moment-river-REBORN-Israeli-desert-delight-watching-locals-predicted-return.html

There are many pictures of the renewal of the land of Israel. She supplies fruit to many countries, particularly Europe.

SIGN #41

THE SANHEDRIN HAS BEEN REFORMED

Mt 26:59 *Now the chief priests, and elders, and all the council [synhedrion], sought false witness against Jesus, to put him to death;*

The Sanhedrin [synhedrion] is "a council of rabbis who led the Israelites before and after the destruction of Herod's Temple. It ceased to function in the fifth century AD, but in 2004 a group of orthodox Jewish groups announced that they were re-establishing it." (WOL) Israel has been without a Sanhedrin for 1500 years.

The "council" is mentioned 22 times in the New Testament. In Jerusalem, it is composed of 71 Jewish leaders and the high priest (72 total). Before Jerusalem was conquered by the Romans, the council had the authority to sentence an individual to death. But when Pilate was ruling, he ordered the death of Jesus at their request. Outlying cities in Israel had a smaller "Sanhedrin." The recently reconstituted council will be functional again when the Antichrist is revealed and the "contract" to protect Israel is signed at the beginning of the 70th week.

SIGN #42

THE FAULT LINE IN THE MOUNT OF OLIVES

***Zec 14:4** And his feet shall stand in that day upon the mount of Olives, which is before Jerusalem on the east, and the mount of Olives shall <u>cleave in the midst thereof toward the east and toward the west,</u> and there shall be a very great valley; and half of the mountain shall remove toward the north, and half of it toward the south.*

SIGN #43

THE DEAD SEA IS CHANGING

Zec 14:8 And it shall be in that day, that <u>living waters</u> shall go out from Jerusalem; half of them toward the former sea, and half of them toward the hinder sea: in summer and in winter shall it be. [The waters of the Dead Sea cannot support life because of the mineral content, but that is changing.]

This article popped up when researching "signs." "Fulfillment of the Dead Sea Prophecy Has Begun"

Before Sodom and Gomorrah were destroyed the region was well watered and gardens were there.

Ge 13:10 And Lot lifted up his eyes, and beheld all the plain of Jordan, that it was well watered every where, before the LORD destroyed Sodom and Gomorrah, even as the garden of the LORD, like the land of Egypt, as thou comest unto Zoar.

But look what is happening: "The water level at the Dead Sea has been receding at the fantastic rate of up to one meter every year. This is due to water being diverted from the Jordan River for agricultural purposes and evaporation caused by the Dead Sea mineral works. The dropping water level has led to sinkholes appearing on the shores of the Dead Sea. On a visit to the arid region, Siegel discovered that many of these pools have been filling up with sweet fresh water, and even more incredibly, fish."
[https://www.breakingisraelnews.com/72711/fulfillment-dead-sea-prophecy-begun/ accessed 12/2018]

SIGN #44

THE FALSE REPLACEMENT THEOLOGY

Ro 9:26-27 And it shall come to pass, that in the place where it was said unto them, Ye are not my people; there shall they be called the children of the living God. 27 Esaias also crieth concerning Israel, Though the number of the children of Israel be as the sand of the sea, a remnant shall be saved: Ro 11:26 And so <u>all Israel shall be saved: as it is written</u>, There shall come out of Sion the Deliverer, and shall turn away ungodliness from Jacob: Ro 11:27-28 For this is my covenant unto them, when I shall take away their sins. 28 As concerning the gospel, they are enemies for your sakes: but as touching the election, they are beloved for the fathers' sakes.

The teaching of Replacement Theology (RT) which proclaims the church replaced Israel, is rampant in the world. From the verses above, it would require a twisting of Scripture to teach RT. One well-known preacher, John Piper, teaches RT. [https://www.h4cblog.com/john-piper-and-replacement-theology, accessed 12/2018] On this webpage, many others are listed who teach similar theology. This "sign" relates to the abandonment of clear statements of Scripture.

SIGN #45
RAMPANT SEXUAL IMMORALITY

2Ti 3:1-4 This know also, that in the last days perilous times shall come. 2 For men shall be lovers of their own selves, covetous, boasters, proud, blasphemers, disobedient to parents, unthankful, unholy, 3 <u>Without natural affection</u>, trucebreakers, false accusers, incontinent, fierce, despisers of those that are good, 4 Traitors, heady, highminded, <u>lovers of pleasures</u> more than lovers of God;

This is a headline that just arrived as I was getting ready to complete this "sign." "Hundreds of Sex Abuse Allegations found in Fundamental Baptist Churches Across US." The article details many instances of sexual abuse. [Miami Herald, Sarah Smith Dec. 9, 2018] However, the accusation is not limited to Fundamental Churches. As a matter of fact, sickening reports relate to the homosexuality and pedophilia found in the Roman Catholic priesthood. Just do a little research. The news headlines about this unrighteousness has been relentless. Examine the CDC reports of sexually transmitted diseases and antibiotic resistance.

SIGN #46
MARRIAGE WOULD BE DISDAINED

Ge 1:27 So God created man in his own image, in the image of God created he him; male and female created he them. Mt 19:4-6 And he answered and said unto them, Have ye not read, that he which made them at the beginning made them male and female, 5 And said, For this cause shall a man leave father and mother, and shall cleave to his wife: and they twain shall be one flesh? 6 Wherefore they are no more twain, but one flesh. What therefore God hath joined together, let not man put asunder. Mr 10:6-7 But from the beginning of the creation God made them male and female. 7 For this cause shall a man leave his father and mother, and cleave to his wife;

The LGBTQ movement has made a mockery of marriage between a man and a woman. Same-sex marriages have exploded across the world. The acceptance of this travesty has precipitated a push for pedo-marriage and polygamy. Furthermore, "just living together" (not married) is now acceptable. Numerous reports affirm that co-habitating (living together without being married) and then getting married, leads to a higher divorce rate. [See also, Mal. 2:14,15, 1 Cor. 7:2, Heb. 13:4]

SIGN #47

NATIONS PLANNING TO ATTACK ISRAEL

Eze 38:2 Son of man, set thy face against Gog, the land of Magog, the chief prince of Meshech and Tubal, and prophesy against him, Eze 38:4-6 And I will turn thee back, and put hooks into thy jaws, and I will bring thee forth, and all thine army, horses and horsemen, all of them clothed with all sorts of armour, even a great company with bucklers and shields, all of them handling swords: 5 Persia, Ethiopia, and Libya with them; all of them with shield and helmet: 6 Gomer, and all his bands; the house of Togarmah of the north quarters, and all his bands: and many people with thee. Eze 38:9 Thou shalt ascend and come like a storm, thou shalt be like a cloud to cover the land, thou, and <u>all thy bands, and many people with thee</u>. Eze 38:12 To take a spoil, and to take a prey; to turn thine hand upon the desolate places that are now inhabited, and upon the people that are gathered out of the nations, which have gotten cattle and goods, that dwell in the midst of the land.

News reports of the "hate" for Israel by the countries mentioned above and their desire to annihilate the nation abound. They often chant "death to America, Israel and the Jews." Persia is Iran, Gomer is Turkey, Magog is Russia, Togarmah (Armenians & Medes of Media-Persia) is associated with Turkey.

SIGN #48

RUSSIA'S INVOLVEMENT IN THE MIDDLE EAST

*Eze 38:2-4 Son of man, set thy face against <u>Gog</u>, the land of <u>Magog</u>, the chief prince of Meshech and Tubal, and prophesy against him, **3** And say, Thus saith the Lord GOD; Behold, I am against thee, O Gog, the chief prince of Meshech and Tubal: **4** And I will turn thee back, and put hooks into thy jaws, and I will bring thee forth, and all thine army, horses and horsemen, all of them clothed with all sorts of armour, even a great company with bucklers and shields, all of them handling swords:*

Russia, a world power, has been identified by many Bible scholars as Magog (the land) and Gog (the ruler). This nation is intimately involved in the affairs of Persia (Iran) and Syria, located next door to Israel. Russia has built a naval seaport, an airport, and an army base in Syria.

"In September, Russian forces began a controversial air campaign in Syria in an attempt to increase the nation's involvement in the Middle East [ME]. While some leaders have welcomed Russia's increased involvement, many in the west have been skeptical of President Vladimir Putin's motives. As Syrian dictator Bashar al-Assad's position weakens amid an ongoing civil war, Russia has stepped in and with Iran's help is ensuring he stays in power." [https://lawstreetmedia.com/issues/world/russias-role-middle-east/, accessed 12/2018, The article was written on October 20, 2015]

[Search Russia's involvement in the Middle East]

66 SIGNS OF AN IMMINENT MASS DEPARTURE

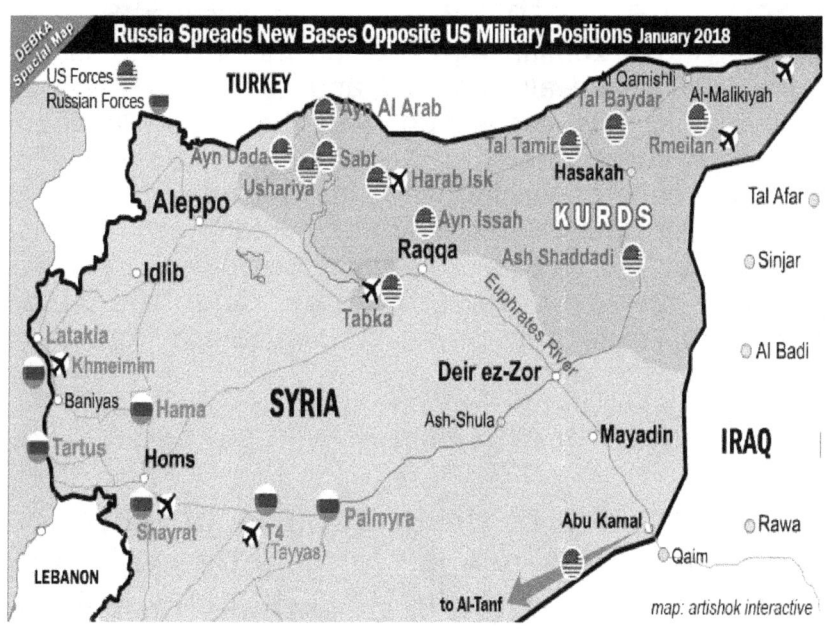

SIGN #49
DAMASCUS WILL BE DESTROYED

Isa 17:1 The burden of Damascus. Behold, Damascus is taken away from being a city, and it shall be a ruinous heap. Isa 17:3 "The fortress also shall cease from Ephraim, and the kingdom from Damascus, and the remnant of Syria: they shall be as the glory of the children of Israel, saith the LORD of hosts.

I have included this as a "sign" because of the constant war presently occurring in Syria where Damascus is located. Hezbollah, a terrorist organization, is associated with Syria. "Israel accused Syria of supplying Hezbollah with Russian-made Scud missiles that can reach all of Israel and can carry chemical weapons. This accusation was made by President Shimon Peres who is known to be a political dove:... Israel sends a warning to Bashar Assad of Syria that it now considers Hezbollah to be military arm of Syria, and that –if Hezbollah attacks Israel – Israel will "return Syria to the Stone Age" and "the Assad dynasty will lose its power and will cease to reign in Syria" [http://www.bereanresearchinstitute.com/04_Endtime/E.0010_001_Damascus_Will_Be_Destroyed.html, accessed 12/2018]

I expect this to occur soon in preparation for the 70th week of Daniel and the Antichrist's endeavor to establish the false peace in Israel.

66 SIGNS OF AN IMMINENT MASS DEPARTURE

SIGN #50
GOD'S PROTECTION OF ISRAEL

Isa 54:15-17 Behold, they shall surely gather together, but not by me: whosoever shall gather together against thee shall fall for thy sake. 16 Behold, I have created the smith that bloweth the coals in the fire, and that bringeth forth an instrument for his work; and I have created the waster to destroy. 17 <u>No weapon that is formed against thee shall prosper;</u> and <u>every tongue that shall rise against thee in judgment thou shalt condemn.</u> This is the heritage of the servants of the LORD, and their righteousness is of me, saith the LORD. Zec 2:5 For I, saith the LORD, will be unto her a wall of fire round about, and will be the glory in the midst of her. Zec 2:8 For thus saith the LORD of hosts; After the glory hath he sent me unto the nations which spoiled you: <u>for he that toucheth you toucheth the apple of his eye.</u>

"There are recent historical examples of God's miraculous protection. As the Jewish State was born in 1948, five Arab armies (Egypt, Syria, Jordan, Lebanon and Iraq) immediately invaded Israel. The Arabs had no difficulty obtaining all the arms they needed. But they were defeated by a fledgling Israeli defense force. Similarly, in the Six-Day War of June 5–10, 1967, the armies of Egypt, Jordan, Syria, Lebanon (and later Iraq) attacked Israel. Their goal was "to wipe Israel off the map". Israel defeated the attack even though the Arab armies had huge superiority in armour, aircraft and troops. And in October 1973 Egypt and Syria launched another attack on Israel (the Yom Kippur War). This was at a time when Israel was "resting" in Yom Kippur. Despite the surprise and consequent losses, Israel once again defeated the attack."

[https://www.factsaboutisrael.uk/god-protects-israel/, Accessed 12/2018] Many many reports

SIGN #51
THE RISE OF ASIA (CHINA)

Re 16:12 And the sixth angel poured out his vial upon the great river Euphrates; and the water thereof was dried up, that the way of <u>the kings of the east</u> might be prepared. *Re 9:16* And the number of the army of the horsemen were two hundred thousand thousand: and I heard the number of them.

John Gill's Exposition of the Entire Bible says: "Two hundred thousand thousand, or two myriads of myriads; two hundred millions, or twenty thousand brigades of ten thousand each...almost infinite and incredible." Hal Lindsey believes the army in Rev. 9 and 16 are the same and is a 200 million strong army: [http://www.freeworldfilmworks.com/dov-200mill2.htm, accessed 12/2018]

There are numerous reports about the growing size and military ability of China. Its ability to form a 200 million strong army from the 1.42 billion population is not presently unrealistic.
[see http://www.pacom.mil/Media/News/News-Article-View/Article/1609684/dod-report-details-chinas-growing-military-economic-power/ accessed 12/2018]

[see http://worldpopulationreview.com/countries/china-population/ accessed 12/2018]

66 SIGNS OF AN IMMINENT MASS DEPARTURE

SIGN #52
SORROWS

Mt 24:4-8 And Jesus answered and said unto them, Take heed that no man deceive you. 5 For many shall come in my name, saying, I am Christ; and shall deceive many. 6 And ye shall hear of wars and rumours of wars: see that ye be not troubled: for all these things must come to pass, but the end is not yet. 7 For nation shall rise against nation, and kingdom against kingdom: and there shall be famines, and pestilences, and earthquakes, in divers places. 8 All these are <u>the beginning of sorrows</u>.

Sorrows "is a period of time characterized by specific **signs** that indicate His return is near. These signs also cause an increase in pain and sorrow that the Bible likens to a woman as she goes through her pregnancy and is about to give birth. The analogy of a pregnant woman to the end times is drawn from Old Testament passages such as <u>Isaiah 13:6-8</u> that describe the Day of the Lord. Prior to a woman giving birth, she experiences painful contractions. The culmination of the sorrows or birth pangs comes at delivery when the pain is most intense. After that, there is joy because of the child that is born! As with a woman about to give birth, the time from the beginning of sorrows until Jesus returns and establishes His eternal kingdom will be characterized by increasing pain and sorrow culminating with utter destruction when God judges the nations and in doing so destroys the beast's (Antichrist's) kingdom." [http://www.thewordonendtimes.com/what-is-the-beginning-of-sorrows/ accessed 12/2018]

The sorrows are specifically: Wars, earthquakes, famines, pestilences, false prophets, persecutions of saints. These have been addressed separately, but the all-inclusive sign is "sorrows."

SIGN #53
POPULATION EXPLOSION

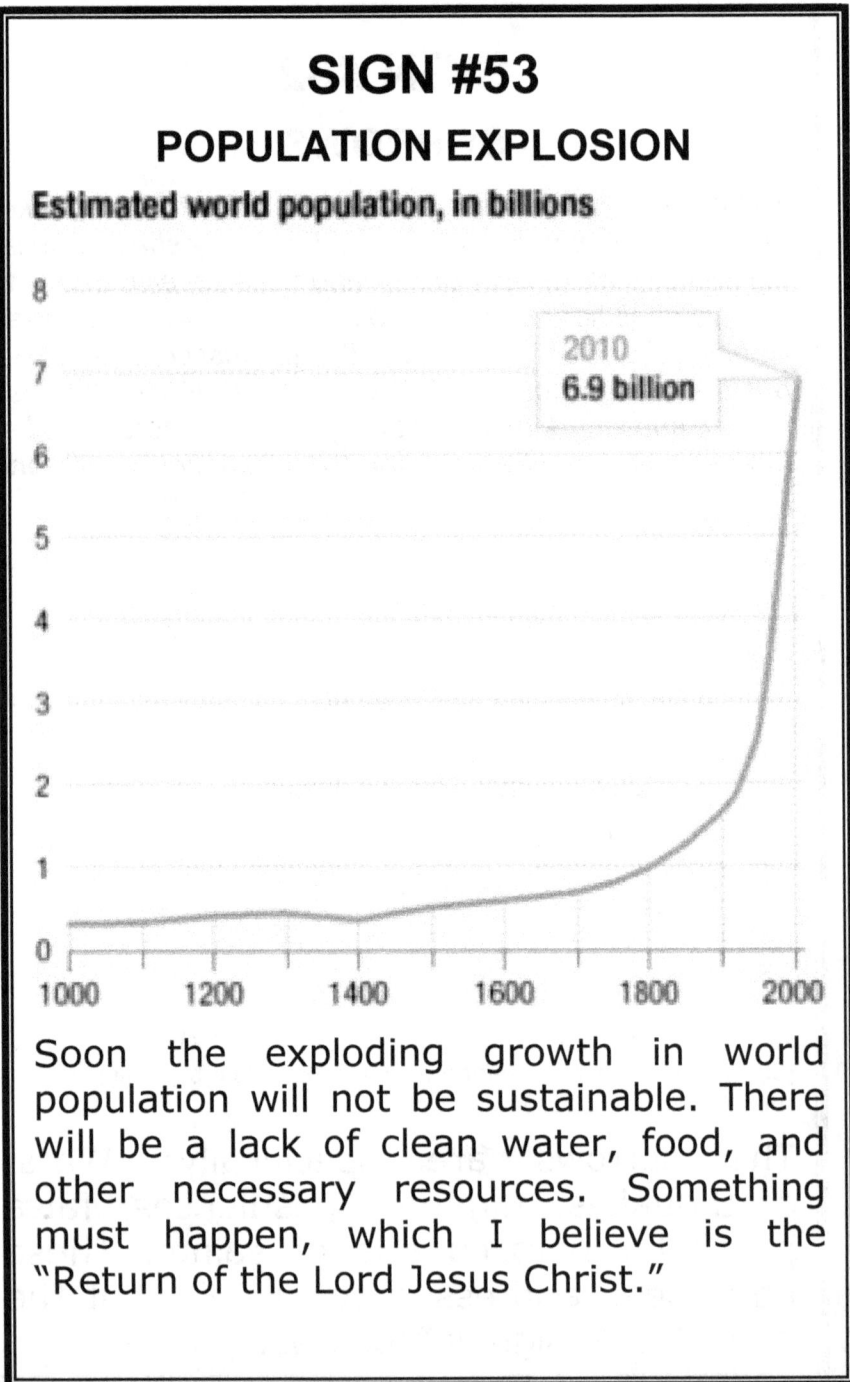

Soon the exploding growth in world population will not be sustainable. There will be a lack of clean water, food, and other necessary resources. Something must happen, which I believe is the "Return of the Lord Jesus Christ."

SIGN #54
IRAN (PERSIA)

Da 8:2-4 *And I saw in a vision; and it came to pass, when I saw, that I was at <u>Shushan</u> in the palace, which is in <u>the province of Elam</u>; and I saw in a vision, and I was by the river of Ulai.* ***3*** *Then I lifted up mine eyes, and saw, and, behold, there stood before the river a ram which had two horns: and the two horns were high; but one was higher than the other, and the higher came up last.* ***4*** *I saw the ram pushing westward, and northward, and southward; so that no beasts might stand before him, neither was there any that could deliver out of his hand; but he did according to his will, and became great.* ***Da 8:17*** *So he came near where I stood: and when he came, I was afraid, and fell upon my face: but he said unto me, Understand, O son of man: for at the time of the end shall be the vision.* ***Da 8:19*** *And he said, Behold, I will make thee know what shall be in the last end of the indignation: for at the time appointed the end shall be.* ***Da 8:26*** *And the vision of the evening and the morning which was told is true: wherefore shut thou up the vision; for it shall be for many days.*

"Shushan, or Susa, the chief town of Susiana, was the capital of Persia after the time of Cyrus, in which the kings of Persia had their principal residence" [Barnes 8:2]

66 SIGNS OF AN IMMINENT MASS DEPARTURE

It is important to recognize Daniel's prophecy does not just depict the days of Alexander the Great or Antiochus in ancient history, but extends to the current day - NOW!

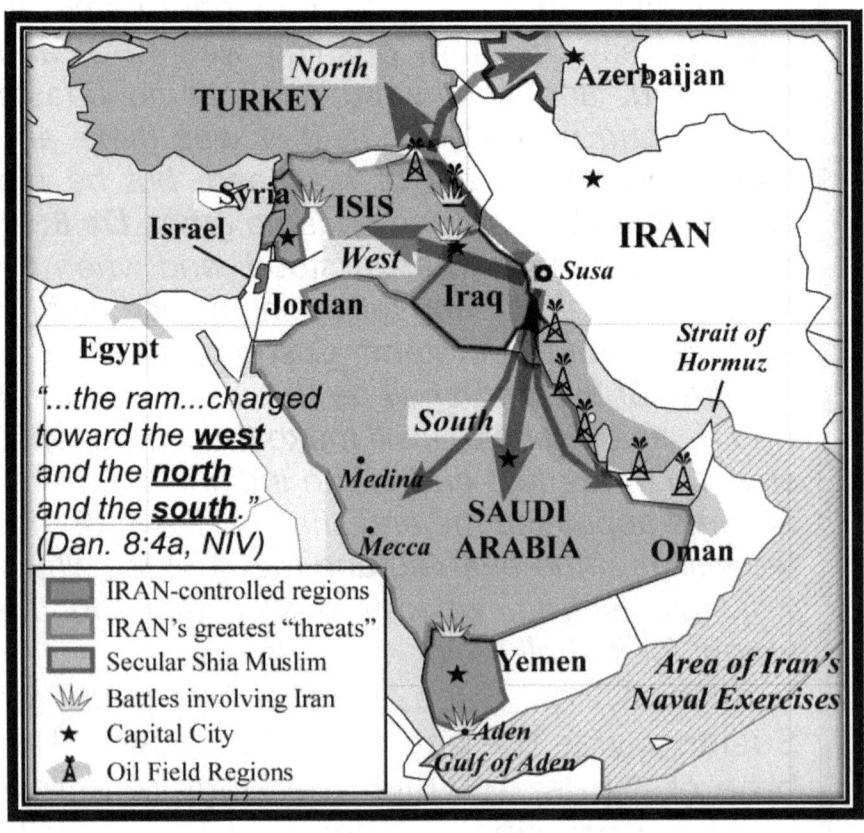

SIGN #55
TURKEY (GOMER)

Eze 38:3-6 And say, Thus saith the Lord GOD; Behold, I am against thee, O Gog, the chief prince of Meshech and Tubal: **4** And I will turn thee back, and put hooks into thy jaws, and I will bring thee forth, and all thine army, horses and horsemen, all of them clothed with all sorts of armour, even a great company with bucklers and shields, all of them handling swords: **5** Persia, Ethiopia, and Libya with them; all of them with shield and helmet: **6** <u>Gomer</u>, and all his bands; the house of <u>Togarmah</u> of the north quarters, and all his bands: and many people with thee.

All of these nations, including Turkey, are aligned against Israel. "[T]today's headlines indicate a marked increase in friction between the nation of Turkey and its supposed ally Israel. As Islamic radicalism has enjoyed political success in recent years, Turkey is becoming more and more anti-Western in its foreign policy. And its hardline Islamic leadership's shared disdain for Israel may well be the deciding factor which drives it into the arms of the Gog/Magog alliance [of Eze. 38:3-6]." [http://www.end-times-bible-prophecy.com/turkey-in-bible-prophecy.html accessed 12/2018]

As I was preparing this "sign," an article suddenly came into my email box. The title was: "Islamic Beast? Turkey Wants Global Islamic Union Governed By Sharia" [http://prophecynewswatch.com/article.cfm?recent_news_id=2834#Ql5Tqg0gk5OzZ7h4.99, accessed 12/2018]

SIGN #56

LITERAL FULFILLMENT OF PROPHECIES

Ro 9:4 Who are Israelites; to whom pertaineth the adoption, and the glory, and the covenants, and the giving of the law, and the service of God, and the promises;

In these last days, you would have to be blind not to see and understand the literal fulfillment of prophecies in Scripture, particularly in relation to the Lord Jesus Christ and Israel. For example, the literal fulfillment of **Mic 5:2**

But thou, Beth-lehem Ephratah, though thou be little among the thousands of Judah, yet out of thee shall he come forth unto me that is to be ruler in Israel; whose goings forth have been from of old, from everlasting.

And **Isa 66:8** *Who hath heard such a thing? who hath seen such things? Shall the earth be made to bring forth in one day? or shall a nation be born at once? for as soon as Zion travailed, she brought forth her children.*

For a complete review of these things, see Dr. Dwight Pentecost's book, "Things To Come," which goes into great detail with many examples. Also, "Evidence That Demands a Verdict" by Josh McDowell.

SIGN #57
SIGNS IN THE HEAVENS

Lu 21:25-26 *And there shall be signs in the sun, and in the moon, and in the stars; and upon the earth distress of nations, with perplexity; the sea and the waves roaring; 26 Men's hearts failing them for fear, and for looking after those things which are coming on the earth: for the powers of heaven shall be shaken.* **Mt 24:29** Immediately after the tribulation of those days shall <u>the sun be darkened, and the moon shall not give her light,</u> and the stars shall fall from heaven, and the powers of the heavens shall be shaken:

"Many people today believe that these celestial signs are only starting to be fulfilled in our day, with such events like solar flares that occur in the sun and the 'blood moon(s)'. But the truth is, the Bible verses in Matthew and Luke where Jesus talks about celestial signs in the stars, sun and moon have <u>already been fulfilled</u>. Sure, there will be disturbances in the heavens as we near the very last days, but this particular prophecy of the sun, moon and stars in Matthew and Luke has already been fulfilled. And this is yet more evidence that we *are* living in the end times.

On May 19th in 1780 a dark day occurred in New England in America. **This dark day covered the New England states and parts of Canada**. The darkness was observed as far north as Portland, Maine, and extended south to New Jersey. And the daytime darkness was so complete that candles were required from noontime that day until the middle of the next night. *"Three centuries ago in parts of North America, a strange event turned morning to night.* <u>***It remains wreathed in mystery***</u> *- so what caused the Dark Day? The Dark Day, as it's become known, took place on May 19, 1780 in New England and parts of eastern Canada. For the past 232 years historians and scientists have argued over the origins of this strange event."* (bbc news - source)" [http://www.signs-of-end-times.com/celestial-signs-sun-stars-moon.html. accessed 12/20181

SIGN #58

SCOFFERS MOCKING THE 2ND COMING

2Pe 3:3-4 *Knowing this first, that there shall come <u>in the last days</u> <u>scoffers</u>, walking after their own lusts, **4** And saying, Where is the promise of his coming? for since the fathers fell asleep, all things continue as they were from the beginning of the creation.*

Dr. D. Cloud reports that "The scoffing began in earnest in the 19th century. Before that, most men in the West believed in divine creation. That century witnessed the following: an explosion of skepticism; the birth of theological modernism, humanistic philosophy, textual criticism, Unitarianism, Marxism, Darwinism, Mormonism, Jehovah's Witness, Seventh-day Adventism, Psychology, New Age...."

"Attendance at places of worship is declining and reverence for holy things is vanishing. We solemnly believe this to be largely attributable to **THE SCEPTICISM WHICH HAS FLASHED FROM THE PULPIT AND SPREAD AMONG THE PEOPLE**" (C.H. Spurgeon, *Sword and Trowel*, November 1887).

[https://www.wayoflife.org/reports/modern_scoffers_prove_bible_is_true.html, accessed 12/2018]

SIGN #59

EXPLOSION IN WITCHCRAFT

Ga 5:19-20 Now the works of the flesh are manifest, which are these; Adultery, fornication, uncleanness, lasciviousness, 20 Idolatry, <u>witchcraft</u>, hatred, variance, emulations, wrath, strife, seditions, heresies, **2Ti 3:1** *This know also, that in the last days perilous times shall come.* **Jude 17-19** *But, beloved, remember ye the words which were spoken before of the apostles of our Lord Jesus Christ; 18 How that they told you there should be mockers in the last time, who should walk after their own ungodly lusts. 19 These be they who separate themselves, sensual, having not the Spirit.*

Witchcraft has been recognized as a "religion" by the US armed forces. "Department of Defense adds Heathen and Pagan Religions to Recognized Faith Groups" [https://wildhunt.org/2017/04/department-of-defense-adds-heathen-and-pagan-religions-to-recognized-faith-groups.html, accessed 12/2018]

See this: "Narcissism, Witchcraft, and the Last Days" [https://www.shoutingfromtherooftop.com/narcissism-witchcraft-and-the-last-days.html, accessed 12/2018]

Many evils are associated with witchcraft, which is exploding in these last days.

SIGN #60
REVIVAL OF THE HEBREW LANGUAGE

Zep 3:8-9 Therefore wait ye upon me, saith the LORD, until the day that I rise up to the prey: for my determination is to gather the nations, that I may assemble the kingdoms, to pour upon them mine indignation, even all my fierce anger: for all the earth shall be devoured with the fire of my jealousy. **9** For then will I turn to the people a **pure language**, that they may all call upon the name of the LORD, to serve him with <u>one consent</u>.

"The process of the Hebrew language revival began on October 13th 1881, as Eliezer Ben-Yehuda and his friends agreed to exclusively speak Hebrew in their conversations. As a result, the language, which had not been spoken as a mother tongue since the second century CE, once again became the national language of Israel. Some three thousand years earlier, when the Jewish people first arrived in Israel with Joshua, Hebrew was established as the national language and lasted for more than a millennium, until the Bar Kohba war in 135 CE. From that point on, Hebrew was exclusively used for literature and prayer, until late in the 19th century with the first aliya and Ben-Yehuda." [https://www.jpost.com/Jewish-World/Jewish-News/This-week-in-history-Revival-of-the-Hebrew-language, accessed 12/2018]

SIGN #61

CALLING EVIL GOOD AND GOOD EVIL

***Isa 5:18-21** Woe unto them that draw iniquity with cords of vanity, and sin as it were with a cart rope: **20** Woe unto them that <u>call evil good, and good evil;</u> that put darkness for light, and light for darkness; that put bitter for sweet, and sweet for bitter! **21** Woe unto them that are wise in their own eyes, and prudent in their own sight! **Isa 5:22-23** Woe unto them that are mighty to drink wine, and men of strength to mingle strong drink: **23** Which justify the wicked for reward, and take away the righteousness of the righteous from him!*

Using or abusing substances such as marijuana, hallucinogens, alcohol and other drugs is called good by many in these last days. Fornication such as premarital sex, LGBTQ, gender confusion, and other humanistic abominations are called good in these last days. Violence is called good. Blasphemy is called good. Declaring many ways to heaven is called good (but see John 14:6). Deceiving (lying) and being deceived is called good. Adultery is called good by many. Premarital sex is called good by most. Pragmatism is called good. Self-centeredness and self-esteem is called good...

SIGN #62
DRUGS

1Co 6:19 What? know ye not that <u>your body is the temple of the Holy Ghost</u> which is in you, which ye have of God, and ye are not your own?
2Co 1:22 Who hath also sealed us, and given the earnest of the Spirit in our hearts.

Eph 1:13 In whom ye also trusted, after that ye heard the word of truth, the gospel of your salvation: in whom also after that ye believed, ye were sealed with that holy Spirit of promise,

A <u>believer's</u> body is "the temple of God," God's dwelling place on Earth in this dispensation. In these last days, so many have defiled it with addictive substances. The English Scripture translates a Greek Word, pharmakeia = pharmacy or pharmaceuticals, as sorceries, or witchcraft. (Gal. 5:20, Rev. 9:21,23). Consider also sobriety and alcohol, a drug, as considered in the Bible. The Bible is clear: no alcohol, not even a drop. No one can deny the substance abuse <u>epidemic</u> around the world. A sign of the end.

"In 2015, there were 39.7 deaths per 100,000 U.S. residents due to drugs, alcohol and suicide compared with 23.1 in 1999 — a whopping increase of 72%. That number could go up to 56 deaths per 100,000 residents in 2025, said the report commissioned by the Trust for America's Health and the Well Being Trust."

[https://www.usatoday.com/story/news/2017/11/21/deaths-drugs-alcohol-and-suicide-could-hit-1-6-m-over-next-decade-report-says/880887001/, accessed 12/2018]

66 SIGNS OF AN IMMINENT MASS DEPARTURE

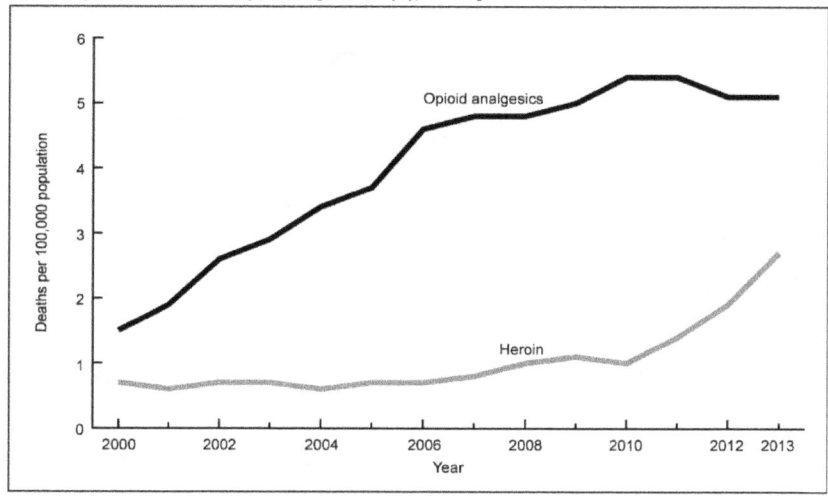

Figure 1. Age-adjusted rates for drug-poisoning deaths, by type of drug: United States, 2000–2013

"NOTES: The number of drug-poisoning deaths in 2013 was 43,982, the number of drug-poisoning deaths involving opioid analgesics was 16,235, and the number of drug-poisoning deaths involving heroin was 8,257. A small subset of 1,342 deaths involved both opioid analgesics and heroin. Deaths involving both opioid analgesics and heroin are included in both the rate of deaths involving opioid analgesics and the rate of deaths involving heroin. Access data table for Figure 1[PDF - 86KB].

SOURCE: CDC/NCHS, National Vital Statistics System, Mortality."

Many sad stats on the webpage to follow:

[https://www.cdc.gov/nchs/data/databriefs/db190_fig1.png, accessed 12/2018]

SIGN #63
GLOBAL BLASPHEMERS

2Ti 3:1-4 *This know also, that <u>in the last days</u> perilous times shall come. 2 For men shall be lovers of their own selves, covetous, boasters, proud, <u>blasphemers</u>, disobedient to parents, unthankful, unholy, 3 Without natural affection, trucebreakers, false accusers, incontinent, fierce, despisers of those that are good, 4 Traitors, heady, highminded, lovers of pleasures more than lovers of God;*

Blasphemers are impious, scurrilous, railing, contemptuous, speaking evil, and irreverent (against God) with the characteristics listed in the verses above. Blasphemy and hate speech laws exist in many countries, but they pale in comparison to the real blasphemy in the hearts of most people.

Mr 3:28-29 *Verily I say unto you, All sins shall be forgiven unto the sons of men, and blasphemies wherewith soever they shall blaspheme: 29 But he that shall blaspheme against the Holy Ghost hath never forgiveness, but is in danger of eternal damnation: (cf., Mat. 12:32).*

As we enter the last days, the world is full of blasphemers, [see humanists, atheists, secularists]...

66 SIGNS OF AN IMMINENT MASS DEPARTURE

Blasphemy Day, also known as International Blasphemy Day or International Blasphemy Rights Day, educates individuals and groups about blasphemy laws and defends freedom of expression, especially the open criticism of religion which is criminalized in many countries. Blasphemy Day was introduced as a worldwide celebration by the Center for Inquiry in 2009. The Center for Inquiry (CFI) is a nonprofit educational organization. Its primary mission is to foster a secular society based on science, reason, freedom of inquiry, and humanist values.[1] CFI has headquarters in the United States and a number of locations around the world.

SIGN #64
DEMONIC EXPLOSION

2Th 2:7 For the mystery of iniquity doth already work: only he who now letteth [restrains] will let, until he be taken out of the way.

Re 16:13-14 And I saw three <u>unclean spirits</u> like frogs come out of the mouth of the dragon, and out of the mouth of the beast, and out of the mouth of the false prophet. 14 For they are the <u>spirits of devils</u>, working miracles, which go forth unto the kings of the earth and of the whole world, to gather them to the battle of that great day of God Almighty.

'Supernatural' events terrify police while interrogating celebrity medium John of God over sexual abuse claims as computer 'takes on life of its own' and electrical appliances short circuit. Spiritual healer Joao Teixeira de Faria, 76, has been accused of sexual abuse. Around 300 other women have claimed Faria has sexually assaulted them. Police questioning Faria said electrical items began to malfunction in the room

The man is called "John of God."
[https://www.dailymail.co.uk/news/article-6511201/Supernatural-events-terrify-police-interrogating-celebrity-medium-sexual-abuse-claims.html, accessed 12/2018]

When the "restrainer" is removed, demonic activity will explode.

66 SIGNS OF AN IMMINENT MASS DEPARTURE

SIGN #65
LGBTQ AGENDA

Ro 1:24-27 Wherefore God also gave them up to uncleanness through the lusts of their own hearts, to dishonour their own bodies between themselves: **25** Who changed the truth of God into a lie, and worshipped and served the creature more than the Creator, who is blessed for ever. Amen. **26** For this cause God gave them up unto vile affections: for even their women did change the natural use into that which is against nature: **27** And likewise also the men, leaving the natural use of the woman, burned in their lust one toward another; men with men working that which is unseemly, and receiving in themselves that recompence of their error which was meet. [see Lev. 18:22] 2Th 2:7 For the mystery of iniquity doth already work: only he who now letteth will let, until he be taken out of the way.

A Self-Styled 'Gay Revolutionary' Offers a Challenge to Straight America: "We shall sodomize your sons, emblems of your feeble masculinity, of your shallow dreams and vulgar lies. We shall seduce them in your schools, in your dormitories, in your gymnasiums, in your locker rooms, in your sports arenas, in your seminaries, in your youth groups, ...wherever men are with men together. Your sons shall become our minions and do our bidding. They will be recast in our image. They will come to crave and adore us. All churches who condemn us will be closed. Our holy gods are handsome young men. ...We shall be victorious because we are fueled with the ferocious bitterness of the oppressed..."

Michael Swift - Boston Gay Community News - February 15-21, 1987 (From the Traditional Values Coalition Special Report, Vol. 18., No. 10)

[http://www.truenews.org/Homosexuality/real_agenda.html, accessed 12/2018]

SIGN #66

WARS AND RUMOURS OF WARS

Mt 24:6 *And ye shall hear of <u>wars and rumours of wars:</u> see that ye be not troubled: for all these things must come to pass, but the end is not yet.*

Jas 4:1 *From whence come wars and fightings among you? come they not hence, even of your lusts that war in your members? [see Mr. 13:7, Lk. 21:9]*

It has become more and more clear that some of the prophecies in Scripture can be fulfilled by atomic/hydrogen bombs (see Eze. 12:14). Here is a headline from this morning's news: "Putin issues ominous warning on rising nuclear war threat." The article said, "Speaking at his annual news conference, Putin warned that "it could lead to the destruction of civilization as a whole and maybe even our planet."

[https://apnews.com/deaa45c70d3c4da98410d5a3ec309510, accessed 12/2018]

Recently numerous TV programs have occurred reporting on electromagnetic pulse (EMP) bombs and their danger.

Wars have occurred down through the centuries, and recent stats indicate wars on every continent. Many maps available on the web. **God's Words are TRUE.**

ABOUT THE AUTHOR

Dr. Williams was born in Ft. Pierce, Florida, July 11, 1941. He was saved at the age of fourteen at his local Baptist church under Pastor J. R. White where he was active in the church youth group. His local church ordained him to preach the gospel. After graduating with honors from high school, he attended Stetson University where he met his wife, Patricia, and they were married in 1961. Starting in the ministerial program at Stetson and switching to pre-med in his junior year, he graduated with honors with a B.A. After Stetson, he taught high school at Eau Gallie, Florida for two years, and then continued his training at the University of Miami Medical School where he graduated with honors and induction into the AOA medical honorary in his junior year. Following his medical training, Dr. Williams and Patricia settled in New Port Richey, Florida where he practiced Family Medicine as a board-certified family practitioner and was a board-certified emergency room physician. He was active in his community as a hospital board member for twenty years, a chief-of-staff, president of the medical society, an advisory board member and president of Moody Bible Institute's Florida program, a board member of the Health Planning Commission, and a teacher at his local Baptist church. He helped

66 SIGNS OF AN IMMINENT MASS DEPARTURE

develop and administrate a multi-specialist medical clinic with forty thousand patients and seventeen doctors. He served as Company Commander of a medical unit in the Florida National Guard for nine years. His Biblical training was obtained at Stetson University, Moody Bible Institute, and Louisiana Baptist University. After retirement, Dr. Williams has continued serving the Lord Jesus Christ as an associate pastor, a teacher, a previous vice-president and representative for the Dean Burgon Society, and a member of the King James Bible Research Council. He received a Ph.D. from Louisiana Baptist University. He has traveled to many foreign lands where he has represented the Dean Burgon Society, has taught courses to pastors and has participated in evangelistic events. He is author of the several books, *The Lie That Changed The Modern World; The Miracle of Biblical Inspiration; Word-For-Word Translating of the Received Texts, Verbal Plenary Translating; Hearing the Voice of God; The Septuagint is a Paraphrase; The Pure Words of God; The Attack on the Canon of Scripture; Origin of the Critical Text; Wycliffe Controversies;* and *The Covenant of Salt, The King James Bible's Accuracy & Faithfulness* in addition to many articles and booklets. Some of his articles can be reviewed at this web address:

http://www.theoldpathspublications.com/TOPArticles.html.

Dr. Williams and his wife, Patricia have two sons, five grandchildren, and nine great-grandchildren. They recently celebrated their 57th wedding anniversary. He and his wife are the Directors of The Old Paths Publications, which

66 SIGNS OF AN IMMINENT MASS DEPARTURE

specializes in print-on-demand (POD) books. The purpose of their endeavor is to help authors of Biblically sound books make their works available to the public by reducing the upfront costs of printing, storing, and shipping books by printing the books in the US, England (EU), Australia, and by affiliate printers in many nations, and by making the books available by many distributors such as Amazon worldwide, Barnes and Noble, and others.

www.ingramcontent.com/pod-product-compliance
Lightning Source LLC
Chambersburg PA
CBHW060817050426
42449CB00008B/1703